Living with Hearing Loss

Living with Hearing Loss

Marcia B. Dugan

Gallaudet University Press

Washington

Gallaudet University Press
Washington, DC 20002

http://gupress.gallaudet.edu

Library of Congress Cataloging-in-Publication Data

Dugan, Marcia B.
    Living with hearing loss / Marcia B. Dugan.
        p. cm.
    ISBN 1-56368-134-X
    1. Deafness.   2. Hearing disorders.   3. Hearing aids.   I. Title.

RF290 .D84 2003
362.1'978—dc21   2002068988

Contents

Foreword   ix

Preface   xi

Acknowledgments   xiii

1   Hearing Loss: The Early Signs   1

2   What Is Hearing Loss?   4

3   Myths about Hearing Loss: Fact and Fiction   7

4   How Your Hearing Loss Affects Your Family and Friends   11

5   How the Ear Works   14

6   Types of Hearing Loss   17

7   Causes of Hearing Loss   20

8   Effect of Medication on Hearing Loss   22

9   Noise   25

10   Tinnitus   27

11   What to Do If You Suspect a Hearing Loss   32

12   Understanding Your Hearing Evaluation   34

13   Choosing a Hearing Aid Dispenser   39

14   Will a Hearing Aid Help?   41

15   Types of Hearing Aids   43

16   The Importance of Fitting Hearing Aids   49

17 Purchasing a Hearing Aid   52

18 When Hearing Aids Are Not Enough   57

19 Hearing the Doorbell, Telephone, and Fire Alarm   66

20 Hearing on the Telephone   69

21 Cochlear Implants   76

22 Speechreading   80

23 Will an Oral Interpreter Help?   82

24 Assertive Communication   85

25 Tips for Improving Communication   88

26 Rearranging Your Home Environment   91

27 Living Alone   93

28 The International Symbol of Access for Hearing Loss   97

29 What Are Your Legal Rights?   98

30 Hearing in Restaurants   102

31 Hearing in Theaters and Movies   106

32 Hearing in Places of Worship   109

33 Hearing in the Hospital   111

34 Hearing When Traveling   117

35 Hearing in the Courtroom   122

36 Volunteering or Returning to Work   125

37 A New Friend: The Internet   128

38 Hearing Loss and Eldercare   132

39 Overcoming Psychosocial Effects of
   Hearing Loss   135

40 Healthy Living/Managing Stress   141

41 What Is SHHH?   147

42 Some Final Words   150

   Glossary   153

   Appendix A: Information Resources on
   Hearing Loss   161

   Appendix B: Statistics on Hearing Loss in
   the Aging Population   169

   Index   171

Foreword

WHY IS IT that people with developing hearing loss take as many as seven years to seek help? Stigma is still a valid answer. Hearing loss, often associated with aging in a youth-oriented society, is seen as an embarrassment. In addition to stigma and possible denial, lack of information about hearing loss and how and where to seek help is certainly high on the list of why people don't get help.

Marcia Dugan takes a giant step toward filling the information gap with her excellent book *Living with Hearing Loss*. Armed with intelligence and sensitivity as her base and her long experience as a person with hearing loss, as well as her close association with some of our better professionals in the field, she has the credentials to produce such a fine piece of work. The icing on the cake is her experience with Self Help for Hard of Hearing People (SHHH). In her capacity as a former national board member and president of SHHH, she has one of the best resources in the country at her disposal. Her attentive interactions with hundreds of people with hearing loss give her many of the insights she shares in this book.

These unique circumstances have allowed Marcia Dugan the opportunity to provide us with accurate information on the causes, implications, and possible solutions of hearing loss. What makes this book different from many of the books published on this subject during the last two decades becomes clear early in the book. She writes *for* the consumer with the mind and heart of a consumer. Well-organized, easy to read, and eminently practical, she covers all the bases and leaves little reason to delay further in taking immediate steps to get your hearing under control. She has given us a gift that is of value to anyone with a hearing loss, as well as family and friends.

So often it is difficult to explain what the problem is to our friends and associates. No more! Read this book and you will be equipped with the information you need, as well as the increased confidence to use it. Those of us who have a hearing loss owe a great debt of thanks to Marcia Dugan, her publisher, and SHHH, for this truly helpful book.

Howard E. "Rocky" Stone
Founder and Executive Director Emeritus, SHHH

Preface

It is difficult for people who do not have a hearing loss to understand what a hard of hearing person experiences. Many people who hear well think that all you have to do is turn up the volume and ask others to speak louder.

The real problem with hearing loss, however, is that it often creates a barrier to communication. It can prevent a person from having normal conversations with family and friends, in the workplace, and on the telephone; enjoying TV, the movies, theater, and music; and participating in public activities, meetings, and group assemblies.

Older Americans don't have to give up the lifestyle they enjoy if they acknowledge their hearing loss, seek information, and learn how they can help themselves; however, they often delay in learning to live with their hearing loss. Many retire early because of the stresses of working in a job setting with no accommodations for their disability. Others have health conditions that take precedence over doing something about their hearing loss. It is also sad that older people with hearing loss often are targeted by mail order hearing aid sales and other marketing schemes at a time when many live on limited or fixed incomes.

The information in this book reflects my own experience with hearing loss and the knowledge I acquired while finding out what to do about it in order to remain in the mainstream. It was written to help you learn to live with your hearing loss. Living with a hearing loss does not mean giving in to it; many communication strategies and assistive devices are available to ease the difficulties of understanding speech. You will find out that a great deal can be done to improve communication, even though your hearing loss cannot be changed.

Confucius said, "The essence of knowledge is, having it, to use it." I hope that readers of this book will use the knowledge gained from reading it to take the steps needed to live better with hearing loss.

Acknowledgments

IT IS WITH a special measure of gratitude that I thank Gallaudet University for its interest in publishing *Living with Hearing Loss*. As a strong believer that many older Americans have the potential to remain active and independent well into their later years, I am pleased to have the opportunity to provide information that can help those with hearing loss to do just that.

The information in the book was gleaned from a broad spectrum of resources: products, promotional materials, and publications, as well as from the experiences of many SHHH members who shared strategies for dealing with situations that often challenge people with hearing loss.

I am especially indebted to a number of people who through their expertise have made this book possible: current and former SHHH National staff members Donna Sorkin, Brenda Battat, and Barbara Harris for helping me develop the concept, reviewing the manuscript, and offering suggestions; members of the SHHH Rochester chapter, whose sharing of personal experiences with hearing loss provided insight and information for the experiential keys; the many contributors to *Hearing Loss: The Journal of Self Help for Hard of Hearing People*, whose articles provided background information; Linda Bement, M.S., CCC-A, Diane Castle, Ph.D., John Niparko, M.D., Mark Ross, Ph.D., and David Baquis for their audiological, technical, and medical expertise; Julie Olson, former president of SHHH, for information regarding psychosocial effects of hearing loss; the writers on my former staff at the National Technical Institute for the Deaf, who wrote many of the brochures and *NTID Focus* articles from which I drew information and whose writing skills educated me; Jorge Samper for creating the illustrations; and very special thank yous to Susan Cergol, writer-editor *sin par*, and dear friend, Janice Ogden, whose suggestions while reviewing the final product permitted me to make it a clearer, better book.

(1)

Hearing Loss: The Early Signs

IT MAY BE difficult to remember the first time you realized that you couldn't hear as well as you once did. Most hearing loss occurs gradually, so you may not even have noticed that it was happening. You could hear some people; you had difficulty hearing others. You could hear in some situations; in other situations, you had a problem hearing. These mixed signals are confusing and often prevent people from acknowledging a hearing loss. For this reason, a friend or family member is often the first person to notice that someone is losing their hearing. Below are some of the warning signs of early hearing loss:

- You hear but cannot understand.
- You ask people to repeat what they said or respond inappropriately to questions.
- You have difficulty understanding in restaurants, the car, and other noisy environments where several people are talking at the same time.
- You have difficulty hearing at the movies or in the theater.
- You have difficulty understanding in group or social situations.
- You can't understand your grandchildren or other young children.
- You hear better in one ear than in the other when you are on the telephone.
- You have dizziness, pain, or ringing in your ears.

- You turn the television and radio volume louder than other people like.
- You have difficulty understanding speech if you can't see the speaker's face.
- You turn your head to one side to hear what is said.

In addition to observing the above signs, your family may notice the following:

- You have a blank expression on your face.
- You speak too loudly or too softly.
- You can't understand what is being said when someone speaks to you from another room.
- You avoid social situations.
- You tune out or fall asleep at group gatherings.

Denial

The average delay between the onset of hearing loss and seeking a professional diagnosis is five to seven years. One reason for this delay is not noticing the change in hearing in the early stages of acquired hearing loss. A more prevalent reason is failing to admit there is a problem or avoiding the problem. If you are in the denial stage, you may try to hide the loss because you perceive it as a sign of aging or carrying the stigma of a disability. You also may hide your hearing loss by not participating in conversations, by smiling when everyone else is doing so, and by bluffing in other ways. Denial is exacerbated by the fact that in some situations you can hear and in others you cannot, so you waver between acceptance and denial of the need for a hearing test. The hearing loss is often obvious to your family members and friends; however, if you are like most hard of hearing people, at first you may blame your problem on others.

It Doesn't Hurt

Since hearing loss is usually free of physical pain, people who are hard of hearing tend to put off dealing with it, especially if they are also experiencing other physical problems such as arthritis and heart disease. Although physically painless, hearing loss can cause you emotional pain since it can make you feel socially inept, isolated, embarrassed, even depressed. Poor hearing disrupts communication and can lead to unhappiness. It also can cause pain for your family and friends who may become frustrated and angry when trying to communicate with you (see chapter 4).

Getting Help: Make It a Priority

If listening situations are causing you to strain, tune out, or feel fatigued and irritable, it may be time to admit you have a hearing loss. If so, this is the time to see a hearing health care specialist to determine what the problem is. Some hearing losses may be medically or surgically correctable; most can be helped by wearing a hearing aid. Much information is available when you decide that doing something about your hearing loss is your top priority.

Maintaining good communication with your family and friends is vital to remaining happy, healthy, and in control of your life. It is especially important for older people. You owe it to yourself to have the best quality of life possible.

(2)

What Is Hearing Loss?

HEARING LOSS often occurs gradually, and you may not be aware that you have not been hearing as well as you once did. You may find you hear well in some situations and wonder why it is difficult for you to understand in others. Your family, friends, and co-workers may often have to repeat themselves so that you can understand them.

Unlike other disabilities, hearing loss is invisible. There are no wheelchairs, leg braces, or red-tipped canes to indicate that a person has a hearing loss. Yet, hearing loss is the most prevalent, least recognized, and least understood physical disability. *One of every ten people has a hearing loss.* And although not normal at any age, hearing loss is more common among older adults than in the general population. At age sixty-five, one in every three people has some degree of hearing loss, and the incidence is even higher among those of more advanced years.*

Although hearing loss will require some changes, by acknowledging it and with help from professionals and technology—as well as self help—you can enjoy an independent and relaxed lifestyle. Like many others, you will discover new ways to adapt in order to fully participate in the world around you.

---

*"Hearing Loss and Older Adults," Bethesda, Md.: National Institute on Deafness and Other Communication Disorders [cited 4 Aug 2002]; available from http://www.nidcd.nih.gov/health/pubs_hb/older.htm.

Remember: The real problem with a hearing loss is not the loss itself, but the barrier to communication it creates and the stress you may experience if you do not address it.

Degrees of Hearing Loss

Just as people have varying degrees of visual problems, individual hearing losses also are different and range from mild to profound (see figure 1). The degree of hearing loss is indicated in decibels (dB), which is a measure of loudness.

- If you have a *mild* hearing loss (26–45 dB), you may have difficulty hearing and understanding someone who is speaking from a distance or who has a soft voice. You also

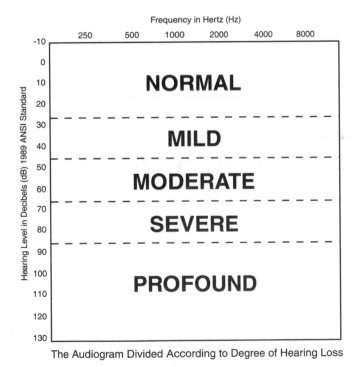

The Audiogram Divided According to Degree of Hearing Loss

Figure 1. Degrees of hearing loss

may have difficulty understanding conversations in noisy backgrounds.

- If your hearing loss is in the *moderate* range (46–65 dB), you will have difficulty understanding conversation in quiet backgrounds as well.
- If your hearing loss is *severe* (66–90 dB), you will have difficulty understanding conversations in all situations.
- If you have a *profound* hearing loss (greater than 90 dB), you may not even hear loud speech or environmental sounds.

But volume is only part of the problem; sounds can also seem distorted. In other words, you can hear, but you cannot understand. This is because hearing loss has two parts: loudness and clarity.

Loudness

A person with a loudness problem usually will find it much easier to understand speech if sounds are made loud enough; some sounds, however, may never be loud enough to be heard.

Clarity

The person with a clarity problem finds sounds are unclear or cannot be understood at all even when amplified. Most hard of hearing people experience problems with both loudness and clarity.

Frequency

Frequency (pitch), which is important for understanding speech, is measured in hertz (Hz). You may have trouble hearing consonants like *s*, *f*, and *th*, but still be able to hear low-frequency sounds such as *ah*, *oo*, and *m*. This is because hearing loss for older people is usually greater in the higher frequencies.

(3)

Myths about Hearing Loss: Fact and Fiction

ONCE YOU have acknowledged your hearing loss and decided to do something about it, you will receive advice—solicited and unsolicited—from family and friends, and even medical personnel.

Some of this advice and information is accurate, but a large amount of misinformation has been circulated over the years. Listed below are some incorrect statements and the corrected information to help you understand your hearing loss.

Myth: A mild hearing loss is nothing to be concerned about.

Truth: Although you may think that you are not missing important information and seem to be managing, you may not realize that your family and friends are frustrated and that you have begun to feel left out. Not only should you be concerned about your hearing loss, you should do something about it.

Myth: You will be the first person to notice that you have a hearing loss.

Truth: Because hearing loss often occurs gradually, you may not notice it at first. Family members and co-workers often are the first to notice that you need to have questions repeated or that the television is too loud.

Myth: Your hearing loss is normal for your age.

Truth: Hearing loss is not normal at any age; however, hearing loss is more prevalent among older adults than in the general population. Currently, approximately one-third of the population older than sixty-five has some degree of hearing loss.

Myth: You have a sensorineural hearing loss (nerve deafness) and there is nothing you can do about it.

Truth: Most hearing losses can be helped with amplification and assistive listening devices. A majority of people with nerve deafness hear better by wearing hearing aids. This form of hearing loss is not correctable with surgery. Conductive hearing loss, however, is often correctable medically or surgically.

Myth: You would understand people if you listened more carefully.

Truth: Although paying attention, watching the speaker's lips, and observing body language can help you understand the message, no amount of careful listening can make you understand what you can't hear clearly. If you have a hearing loss, you need to acknowledge it and see a trained hearing health care professional for an evaluation to determine if you would benefit from a hearing aid.

Myth: Your hearing loss is not bad enough for a hearing aid.

Truth: Everyone's hearing loss is different. Some hard of hearing people hear well on the telephone; others have difficulty. Some have no problem in a quiet one-on-one situation but have difficulty in a noisy or group setting. You must determine the degree of difficulty you are having, and together with a trained hearing health care professional, determine your need for a hearing aid.

Myth: A hearing aid will correct your hearing.

Truth: A hearing aid may be helpful, but it is not a cure for hearing loss. Hearing aids are not like eyeglasses; they cannot correct or restore hearing to normal levels, but they will make sounds louder. If your hearing loss can be helped with a hearing aid, then an appropriately prescribed and fitted hearing aid should make your hearing and understanding abilities better, and in turn, improve your quality of life.

Myth: A hearing aid will damage your hearing.

Truth: A hearing aid will *not* damage your hearing.

Myth: Your hearing loss is not bad enough for two hearing aids.

Truth: We normally hear with two ears; therefore, most people with hearing loss in both ears can understand better with two aids than with one.

Myth: Behind-the-ear hearing aids are old fashioned; you will do much better with the newer in-the-ear hearing aids.

Truth: Behind-the-ear hearing aids are as "state of the art" as in-the-ear hearing aids. Some include features not found in the smaller hearing aids, and a particular feature may be important for you. You should work closely with your hearing health care provider to ensure that the aid you get is appropriate for your particular needs. Function, not appearance, is the crucial consideration.

Myth: You should have your hearing tested in your own home where you spend most of your time.

Truth: The hearing test should be conducted in a sound-proof room in order to provide the most accurate results. The information gleaned from the test is used to select the most appropriate hearing aid for your individual hearing loss. Only individuals confined to a bed for health reasons should have hearing tests in other sites such as their home.

Myth: You can save a lot of money buying a hearing aid through the mail.

Truth: When you buy a hearing aid, you not only are buying a piece of equipment, you are buying the service of a hearing health care provider in your locality. Unlike eyeglasses, hearing aids require a longer period of adjustment and often modifications that can only be made by trained personnel. The wrong hearing aid, or one that is not fitted properly, can be worse than no hearing aid at all.

Myth: Your hearing loss will not change in the future.

Truth: No one can predict the future. Your hearing loss may remain stable for the rest of your life, or it may change slowly and progressively or suddenly and dramatically.

Myth: Learn to speechread (lipread) and you will understand just fine.

Truth: Many people benefit from taking speechreading lessons; however speechreading is not a substitute for hearing aids but a complement to them. Research studies have found that only about three out of ten words can be speechread clearly, only about 30 to 40 percent of speech is visible, and many words that are visible look the same on the lips (for example, *pat* and *bat*, *see* and *tea*).

(4)

How Your Hearing Loss Affects Your Family and Friends

THINK ABOUT the many activities you enjoy with your family and friends and what it would be like to feel left out. Holiday gatherings, where everyone is talking at the same time, can become a frustrating and sad experience for you. While others are enjoying conversing with one another, you are missing out. You want to hear what your family members are talking about but cannot understand them and may have even more difficulty understanding what your grandchildren are saying.

You also may have curtailed other family activities, including movies, watching television, playing cards, and eating out, which once were enjoyable family times, because you don't hear as well as you once did. Traveling, which includes understanding directions, information from tour guides, and conversation with strangers, may become a source of anxiety rather than the fun it is supposed to be. Even conversing while driving a car, something you have enjoyed for years, becomes impossible.

When you lose your hearing, you lose your ability to communicate as easily as you once did. You do not lose your mind, your intelligence, your talent, or your sense of humor. This is important to remember, since the longer you deny you have a hearing loss, the more difficult it will be to maintain the relationships you have had with family and friends.

11

Family and friends are your sources of support. They will be there to work with you and stand by you when you need them, but you need to do your part to earn their love and support.

Bluffing, in an effort to hide your hearing loss, often creates stressful situations for you and your family. When communication breaks down, tension, frustration, and anxiety often result. Misunderstandings occur, which can create problems such as missed appointments and confused directions and other information.

Hearing loss can drive you and your family apart. But it doesn't need to be that way.

What You Can Do

Sit down with family and friends and talk honestly. Admit that you have a hearing loss. Family members may initiate this talk because they noticed the loss before you did. Tell them how you feel about your loss and what they can do to help. Perhaps you are self-conscious, or feel left out. You may be worried about losing even more hearing. You may be concerned about wearing a hearing aid, if a diagnosis suggests this recourse.

If you have not had your hearing loss diagnosed, this should be the first step (see chapter 12). You and your family will want to know what kind of loss you have and what can be done about it. Most families have never dealt with a hearing loss and may have misconceptions about what to do. You and your family should learn about the many things you and they can do together to help you hear better and improve communication at home.

If the diagnosis suggests amplification—and this is not the answer for everyone—see a hearing health care specialist and together decide which is the best hearing aid for you (see chapter 17). You will have taken the first step to improving communication.

You will need your family's support as you adjust to wearing the aid. Often, families think that a hearing aid will restore your hearing to normal. As you learn about the effects of background noise on your ability to hear with and without a hearing aid, you will need to let your family know what you are going through and what they can do to help.

You will need to educate your family about the best environments for communicating with you and changes such as lighting and positioning that should be made to enhance your understanding of speech. You also can give them tips for communicating with you (see chapter 25).

If you are married, your spouse is the person most affected by your hearing loss. Your spouse may have known you when you could hear and may need to be reeducated as to the best way to communicate with you. Spouses will talk to you from another room, talk to your back, and even suggest that "you hear what you want to hear." You will need to be patient as you deal not only with your own hearing loss but your spouse's frustrations as well. Pillow talk, an important part of your relationship, may no longer take place in the dark since you need to see your spouse's face in order to hear. The quality of your relationship will be enhanced as you make concerted efforts to work at communicating better.

It may be easy to let a family member with normal hearing do the talking and thus take over your life, but your quality of life is likely to suffer. Instead, avoid depending on your spouse or other family member by taking charge of the information you want to receive and share with others. Be careful not to confer the role of full-time interpreter on your spouse.

Family members often forget that you don't hear as well as you once did. It is okay to remind them about ways to communicate better. You will need to be patient and understanding but also assertive (see chapter 24). Remember, taking control of your life and your rights without infringing on the rights of others is what honest and assertive communication is all about.

(5)

How the Ear Works

THE HUMAN ear is a delicate and sensitive structure. Under normal conditions it processes a wide range of acoustical activity through the nervous system and the brain in order for you to be able to hear sound.

When any part of the ear breaks down, it affects our ability to perceive sound. Disease, heredity, infections, and noise are among the causes of hearing loss. Aging is another major cause of hearing deterioration.

To understand what happens when our hearing diminishes, you need to understand the anatomy of the ear and how it works.

Anatomy of the Ear

The ear has three major parts: the outer ear, the middle ear, and the inner ear (see figure 2). The outer ear collects sound waves and funnels them into the middle ear, which passes them on to the inner ear. The inner ear converts the waves

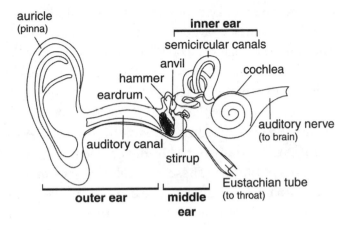

Figure 2. Anatomy of the ear

into nerve impulses and transmits them to the brain. The inner ear also contains the balance mechanism.

- The **outer ear** includes both the ear we see—the pinna—and the outer ear canal, a passage about three quarters of an inch long. Sound travels through the canal and hits the eardrum, a thin membrane that separates the outer ear from the middle ear.
- The **middle ear** is a small cavity between the eardrum and the inner ear. It contains three small, connected bones (ossicles): the malleus (hammer), the incus (anvil), and the stapes (stirrup). When the eardrum vibrates, these bones also vibrate, thus conducting sound to the inner ear. The middle ear also includes the eustachian tube, which leads to the nose and throat, and whose main function is to keep the air pressure in the middle ear equal to the surrounding environment.

- The **inner ear** consists of two structures that contain
  membrane-lined chambers filled with fluid: the labyrinth and the cochlea. The labyrinth is the part of the ear
  used for balance. The cochlea plays a role in hearing.
  The auditory nerve attaches to the labyrinth and the cochlea, and connects the hearing and balance functions of
  the inner ear to appropriate parts of the brain. As sound
  vibrations are transmitted to the cochlea, they set tiny
  hair cells in motion. These hair cells transform the vibrations into nerve impulses. The acoustic nerve picks up
  these impulses and sends them to the brain, which inter-
  prets these signals as words and other sounds.

The labyrinth in each inner ear monitors the position and
movements of the head by means of three semicircular canals. Each canal is at right angles to the other two so that
when you nod, shake, or tilt your head, one or more of the
canals detects the movement and relays the information to
the brain. The brain, in turn, coordinates this information
with your eyes and the muscles in your body to assess your
exact position and the movements you need to make to keep
your balance. When you experience a loss of balance, it usually means that you have a disorder of the inner ear.

Most sound starts outside the ear, causing the air to vibrate
and produce sound waves. The pinna channels the sound
waves down the ear canal to the eardrum, which begins to
vibrate. The vibrations pass through the hammer, anvil, stirrup, and oval window into the cochlea. The tiny hairs in the
cochlea change the vibrations into nerve impulses, which are
transmitted by the auditory nerve to the brain.

You will experience a hearing loss when sound cannot be
transmitted normally through the ear canal because of an

occlusion such as earwax, a perforated eardrum, damaged or defective ossicles, or damaged hair cells. No matter what the nature of your hearing loss, a hearing health care specialist can conduct a painless evaluation and recommend the best treatment.

(6)

Types of Hearing Loss

ONCE YOU are aware that you have a hearing loss, you will want to learn more about it. There are two major types of hearing loss—conductive and sensorineural. Although sensorineural hearing loss is the most prevalent type of loss, especially in older people, you should seek a proper diagnosis from an appropriate hearing health care provider.

Conductive Hearing Loss

Conductive hearing loss is caused by a blockage, usually in the middle ear, that prevents sound from being conducted to the inner ear. The blockage can be caused by wax buildup, an ear infection, fusion of the bones in the middle ear, a punctured eardrum, or tumors. Sounds seem soft but speech is clear as long as it is loud enough. Hearing aids can be very beneficial to people with a conductive loss. This type of hearing loss also often responds to medical or surgical treatment, but only if the auditory nerve and inner ear are functioning well.

Sensorineural Hearing Loss

Sensorineural hearing loss results from damage to the inner ear. The most common cause of sensorineural hearing loss is aging, although high fevers, ototoxic drugs, and noise are other causes. If you have this type of hearing loss, you have trouble hearing in crowded rooms and while watching television, as well as difficulty understanding conversation. Also called *nerve deafness*, this type of hearing loss usually is not caused by damage to the auditory nerve but to the hair cells in the inner ear. Individual hair cells respond, or are "tuned," to specific sounds. Some may be so severely damaged that they cannot react when sound from the outside strikes them. At the same time, the hair cells for certain speech sounds may be functioning normally. This causes you to miss parts of words and sentences. Sensorineural loss is rarely correctable medically or surgically; however, in the great majority of cases, properly fitted hearing aids and assistive devices can help you hear better.

Mixed Hearing Loss

This involves both conductive and sensorineural components. Medical or surgical intervention may help the conductive portion and a hearing aid can help both the sensorineural loss and the conductive component.

Other Hearing Disorders

Other conditions often associated with hearing loss follow.

Tinnitus

Tinnitus is the name for a ringing in the ears or other head noises, a common disorder experienced by nearly 50 million

Americans. Tinnitus, which almost always accompanies a hearing loss, can also affect people with normal hearing (see chapter 10).

Ménière's Disease

One of the more common causes of dizziness (vertigo) is Ménière's disease. Its symptoms also include tinnitus, hearing fluctuation, and hearing loss. Its cause is unknown but probably results from abnormality in the fluids of the inner ear. Currently, no known cure for Ménière's disease is available; however, medications can be prescribed for acute attacks, and symptoms may be prevented or somewhat reduced with certain medications, by adopting a low-sodium diet, avoiding caffeine and alcohol, stopping smoking, avoiding noisy and stressful situations, and using exercise to reduce stress and improve circulation. Sometimes surgery is recommended to relieve acute recurrent attacks of dizziness and severe vertigo.

Autoimmune Inner Ear Disease

Autoimmune Inner Ear Disease (AIED) is treatable especially in its early stages with potent anti-inflammatory medications. The inner ear environment triggers an inflammatory response that can damage components of the hearing and balance receptors within the inner ear. The body itself initiates the inflammatory process, attacking the tissues as foreign, even though there is no infection.

Other Conditions

For information about other conditions associated with hearing loss such as otosclerosis, acoustic neuroma, Usher syndrome, and Cogan syndrome, consult your otolaryngologist and library resources.

(7)

Causes of Hearing Loss

THERE ARE many causes of hearing loss, including

- heredity
- accidents
- diseases such as measles, mumps, and spinal meningitis
- drugs
- noise
- aging

If you recognized your hearing loss when you were fifty-five or older, the most probable cause was age-related hearing loss. Unfortunately, many cases of hearing loss are due to unknown causes. Some of the known causes are explained below.

Heredity

A large proportion of hearing loss that occurs at birth or in the first few years of life is hereditary. Many types of adult-onset and progressive hearing loss are also hereditary. A hereditary (genetic) hearing loss is sometimes easy to identify from family history; a parent or a sibling also may have a loss. In some families, however, the gene that causes hearing loss is recessive, which means the hearing loss may be passed on by parents, even if they themselves do not have a hearing loss.

Accidents

Automobile and work-related accidents can result in head injuries. These injuries, in turn, can cause a dramatic hearing loss. It is usually sudden and traumatic.

Diseases

Diseases such as measles, mumps, and spinal meningitis that are accompanied by high fever have been the cause of hearing loss in many people. These diseases can have indirect consequences as well. For example, when a pregnant woman contracts or is exposed to German measles during the first trimester of pregnancy, there is an increased risk that her child will be born with a hearing loss. The rubella (German measles) epidemic of the mid-1960s caused a significant increase in the number of deaf and hard of hearing people. Since then, vaccinations have greatly reduced the occurrence of these diseases.

Drugs

Some drugs prescribed for medical problems are ototoxic, meaning they have the potential to cause damage to the inner ear, which may result in temporary or permanent hearing loss. If you have a hearing loss, ask your doctor about the medications prescribed for you so that you can prevent an aggravation of your hearing problem (see chapter 8).

Noise

Prolonged exposure to loud noise at or above 90 decibels can damage the sensitive hair cells lining the cochlea. This may cause partial or severe hearing loss. Occupational noise exposure, the most common form of noise-induced hearing loss, threatens the hearing of firefighters, police officers, military personnel, pilots, construction and factory workers, musicians, farmers, and truck drivers, to name a few. Non-occupational sources of hazardous noise such as live or recorded high volume music; recreational vehicles; airplanes; lawn-care equipment; woodworking tools; household appliances such as mixers, blenders, and vacuum cleaners; and chain saws also cause hearing loss. Because no medical or surgical treatment can correct a hearing loss resulting from noise exposure, prevention is important.

Aging

Presbycusis is the term used to describe the slow, progressive type of hearing loss that is associated with aging. At age sixty-five, one out of every three people has a hearing loss. Age-related hearing loss often is due to a lifetime of exposure to dangerous levels of noise or to hereditary adult-onset hearing loss.

(8)

Effect of Medication on Hearing Loss

OTOTOXIC MEDICATIONS are drugs that may cause damage to the inner ear, resulting in temporary or permanent hearing loss and tinnitus. If you have a sensorineural hearing loss, you should ask your doctor and pharmacist about medications prescribed for you since you will want to prevent an aggravation of your hearing problem.

The degree of hearing loss that you experience when taking an ototoxic drug depends on the amount and duration of the use of the medication. If you are taking more than one ototoxic medication, you are even more vulnerable to developing a sensorineural hearing loss or aggravating your existing hearing loss. With many drugs, such as aspirin, hearing loss returns to normal after they are discontinued, no matter how much or how long you use them.

If you experience any of the following signs of ototoxicity, consult your doctor. Some common symptoms are

- noises in your ear (tinnitus)
- pressure in your ears
- an awareness of, and a fluctuation or increase in the degree of your hearing loss
- dizziness

Tell your doctor about your hearing loss and ask if any of the medications prescribed are ototoxic. Ask your pharmacist if any over-the-counter medications you buy have ototoxic effects. Your hearing health care specialist also needs to know about drugs you are taking that may cause fluctuations in your hearing or changes in auditory perception.

Common Ototoxic Medications

Some common ototoxic medications and their effects follow.

Salicylates

The ototoxic effects of aspirin and aspirin-containing products appear after taking six to eight pills per day. Toxic effects are always reversible once medication is discontinued.

Nonsteroidal Anti-Inflammatory Drugs

The ototoxic effects of nonsteroidal anti-inflammatory drugs such as Advil, Clinoril, and Motrin appear after taking six to eight pills per day. Toxic effects are usually reversible once the medication is discontinued.

Antibiotics

Drugs such as streptomycin, erythromycin, and vancomycin when given intravenously are ototoxic. When used topically or administered orally, these drugs are not known to cause hearing loss.

Loop Diuretics

Medications such as Lasix, Edecrin, and Bumex are usually ototoxic when administered intravenously. Ototoxicity is rare when these drugs are given orally.

Chemotherapeutic Agents

Medications such as cisplatin, nitrogen mustard, and vincristine are ototoxic when given for treatment of cancer. The ototoxic effects are enhanced if you are already taking other ototoxic medications such as aminoglycoside antibiotics (streptomycin, kanamycin, neomycin, gentamycin, tobramycin, amikacin, netilmycin) and loop diuretics.

Quinine

The ototoxic effects of drugs containing quinine, such as aralen, atabrine, legatrin, and Q-Vel muscle relaxant, are similar to those of aspirin. The toxic effects are usually reversible once medication is discontinued.

BEING AWARE of ototoxic medications and their early warning signs is important in preserving your residual hearing. If you experience any of the signs of ototoxicity mentioned above, stop the medication immediately and call your doctor.

(9)

Noise

ONE OF THE more frequent complaints made by hard of hearing people is difficulty hearing in noisy surroundings. What may be an acceptable noise level for a person with normal hearing can completely obliterate speech comprehension for someone who is hard of hearing. From this point of view, noise is as much an environmental pollutant as secondary smoke.

Few places exist today that can shield you from loud environmental sounds. Machinery, traffic noise, impact noise, and blast sounds from weapons and detonation exact a heavy toll on the fragile, specialized hair cells within the inner ear. Exposure to excessive noise is a leading cause of hearing loss, and such hearing loss is irreversible.

The first signs of noise-induced hearing loss are typically decreased hearing at higher frequencies (3,000–6,000 Hz), that part of the frequency range in which many of the important consonant sounds lie. You may notice that you cannot distinguish between *back* and *bat* and *flip* and *trip*. With time, noise-induced hearing loss also erodes mid-frequency, and later, low-frequency hearing.

The potential for noise to damage the ear depends on the intensity, tonal qualities, and duration of exposure. The louder, more continuous, and monotonous the noise, the more damage it does. Lawn mowers, leaf blowers, and power saws can cause hearing loss. Common household equipment such as vacuum cleaners and stereos can damage your hearing. Noises in factories, on farms, and on the street can all be harmful to your hearing. Even recreational activities such as hunting, motorcycling, and snowmobiling can cause a loss of hearing.

The effects of moderately loud sounds, such as small engines, can accumulate over years and lead to progressive degeneration of the inner ear's hair cells. Extremely loud sounds, such as the noise from rock concerts, large construction equipment, and blasts, may do damage by tearing delicate inner ear membranes.

If you already have some degree of hearing loss, it is especially important to protect your residual hearing. While it is true that your hearing loss protects you against some loud noises, if the noise is intense enough that it sounds loud to you despite your hearing loss, your ears are probably more sensitive, and you could develop a noise-induced hearing loss. If you know that you are going to be exposed to loud sounds, take no chances—wear hearing protection to avoid further loss.

What else can you do to protect yourself? You can control the noise in your home by turning down the volume on the radio, TV, and stereo, and by using audio headsets only when necessary. You can protect yourself from noise by wearing earplugs, earmuffs, or both. Earplugs can be specially made to custom fit your ear canals, and newer designs let in some speech and music sounds. An audiologist can provide information on the options for hearing protection.

An unwelcome fact is that each day many of us lose a little bit of our ability to hear because of noise surrounding us. In our homes, in the workplace, and on the street, we regularly expose ourselves to dangerous noise levels. In our recreation, too, when we turn to music, one of society's main sources of entertainment, we endanger our hearing by listening to music at dangerously high levels. And as we age, our hearing loss may very well be attributed to a lifetime of exposure to dangerous levels of noise.

(10)

Tinnitus

DO YOUR ears ring, buzz, crackle, or roar? If so, you may be one of the 50 million Americans who experience tinnitus. Tinnitus (pronounced either ti-NIGHT-is or TIN-i-tis) is the medical term for the perception of sound when no external sound is present. It is often referred to as "ringing in the ears," although some people hear hissing, pulsing, clicking, roaring, whistling, chirping, or even voices. The noise can be continuous or fluctuating; it can be tone-like or roaring; it can be simple or complex; it can be in one ear, both ears, or somewhere in the head.

The majority of individuals who suffer from tinnitus are between forty and eighty years of age with prevalence increasing with age. Tinnitus affects women and men equally. Tinnitus can be a minor annoyance that simply becomes background noise, but it also can become an overwhelming problem, interfering with sleep, work, and concentration.

As many as 35 to 45 percent of the adult population and 90 percent of people with hearing loss experience tinnitus at least once in awhile, while somewhere in the vicinity of 1 percent of the population suffers from a chronic tinnitus that has a negative impact on the quality of life. Millions of patients have severe enough tinnitus to seek medical attention. And about 2 million patients are so seriously debilitated that they cannot function on a "normal," day-to-day basis.

Here are a few steps in dealing with tinnitus:

- See an otolaryngologist.
- Consider masking noise to mask your tinnitus.
- Avoid loud noise that is damaging to your ear.
- Keep your blood pressure under control.
- Reduce your salt intake.
- Exercise daily.
- Avoid caffeine and tobacco.
- Avoid medications that cause tinnitus (see chapter 8).

Tinnitus is a symptom, not a disease, the cause of which is not known. There are, however, different ways to classify tinnitus, an important one being *objective* (experienced by the person and the examiner) versus *subjective* (experienced by the person alone). This subjective sensation that only you can hear or measure, and which you perceive to be in your ear, actually occurs in the brain.

What Causes Tinnitus?

The exact physiological cause or causes of tinnitus are not known. There are, however, several likely sources, all of which are known to trigger or worsen tinnitus: noise-induced hearing loss, wax build-up in the ear canal, certain medications, ear or sinus infections, jaw misalignment, cardiovascular disease, certain types of tumors, thyroid disorders, and head and neck trauma.

Exposure to loud noises is by far the most commonly reported cause of tinnitus. The majority of tinnitus patients have some level of noise-induced hearing loss.

Some foods can cause tinnitus. They include cheese, chocolate, Chinese food (MSG), coffee, strong tea, tonic water, red wine, and grain-based spirits. Some people find that foods with high-sugar content or any amount of quinine (such as tonic water) make their tinnitus seem louder.

Some drugs cause tinnitus, while other drugs reportedly make tinnitus worse (see chapter 8).

Finally, stress and fatigue can affect your tinnitus.

Treatment

Just as there is no single cause of tinnitus, there is no cure for tinnitus, but there are treatments that can provide significant relief for many people. The treatments include medication, maskers, changes in lifestyle and diet, and cognitive therapy. In some very limited circumstances surgery can help relieve tinnitus. You will want to talk with your doctor, audiologist, or other health care professional to find the best treatment for you. Because tinnitus is so individual, treatments work differently for different people.

In a limited number of cases, it is possible to determine the cause of tinnitus and to eliminate the tinnitus by eliminating its cause. Unfortunately, this is not possible in most cases. The goal of tinnitus therapy is to minimize the discomfort and disability caused by the tinnitus and to help the individual develop coping strategies.

Drug Therapy

Many drugs have been researched and used as tinnitus relief agents, but no drug will get rid of the problem. Anti-anxiety drugs like Xanax, antidepressants like nortriptyline, antihistamines, anticonvulsants, and even anesthetics like lidocaine have all successfully quieted tinnitus. Because side effects can happen with most drug or drug combinations, you have to decide for yourself if an undesirable side effect is worth the trade off of tinnitus relief.

Masking

Masking devices resemble hearing aids and are designed to produce low-level sound that can reduce and, in some cases, eliminate the perception of tinnitus. Masking can also produce the phenomenon of residual inhibition, where the reduction or elimination of tinnitus perception continues for a short time after the masker is removed.

Hearing Aids

If you have a hearing loss, you might experience total or partial tinnitus relief while wearing hearing aids. There are many variables that determine success. In some cases hearing aids can bring back in the naturally occurring ambient sounds that cover (mask) the tinnitus. When amplified ambient sounds are not sufficient to mask the tinnitus, you may benefit from a unit that combines a hearing aid with a tinnitus masker. Your audiologist can help you decide whether a masker, hearing aid, or combination unit is likely to work best for you.

TMJ Treatment

Tinnitus can be a symptom of a jaw joint (temporomandibular joint, or TMJ) dysfunction because muscles and nerves in the

jaw are closely connected to those in the ear. Dental treatment or bite realignment can help relieve TMJ pain and associated tinnitus. See your dentist if you think you have this
problem.

Biofeedback

Biofeedback training is effective in reducing the intensity of
tinnitus in some people. This training enables you to control
muscle activity in various parts of the body and relax
muscles attached to the head.

Relaxation

Stress and fatigue can affect your tinnitus. Learn to relax. Get
plenty of exercise. Avoid noisy environments that can make
your tinnitus worse. Accept the fact that life events can cause
stress and stress can make your tinnitus worse.

Cognitive Therapy

Cognitive therapy is a type of counseling that is based on
treating a patient's emotional response to tinnitus rather than
treating the tinnitus itself. To accomplish a less negative
emotional response to tinnitus, a counselor will help the
patient identify negative behaviors and thought patterns,
then alter them. Counseling programs are individually
designed for patients and often are most effective when
coupled with other tinnitus treatments such as masking or
medication.

Tinnitus Retraining Therapy

Tinnitus retraining therapy (TRT) combines low-level,
steady background sounds with one-on-one patient/clini-
cian directive counseling. The patient enriches his or her
background sound for a minimum of eight hours a day

usually with in-the-ear sound generators. This combination of therapies helps people habituate (essentially grow unaware of) the sounds of their tinnitus. Tinnitus retraining therapy can take twelve to twenty-four months before a patient no longer needs the in-the-ear devices.

IF CORRECTION of your tinnitus is not possible, it is important for you to learn how to cope with it. An excellent source of information is the American Tinnitus Association (see appendix A).

(11)

What to Do If You Suspect a Hearing Loss

HEARING LOSS is not in itself a disease. It is a symptom of some underlying disorder. Some hearing loss is common as you get older, but if you are under fifty and notice you have a hearing loss, you should see an otolaryngologist or an audiologist, who is trained to identify symptoms that should be treated by a physician. The treatment may be something as simple as flushing out your ears to remove a wax buildup.

If a doctor determines that your hearing loss is not correctable by medication or surgery, you should see a trained specialist for a hearing evaluation. The hearing evaluation will determine if you have a hearing loss, the extent of the loss, and what you can do to hear better.

The person who performs the evaluation is as important as the evaluation itself. You should choose this person carefully (see chapter 13).

There are three kinds of hearing health care providers: otolaryngologists, audiologists, and hearing aid specialists.

Otolaryngologists

Otolaryngologists, or ear, nose, and throat specialists, are physicians who provide medical and surgical treatment for hearing disorders. If your condition cannot be treated medically or surgically, a hearing evaluation is the next step. These physicians do not normally dispense hearing aids; many of them, however, employ audiologists to evaluate your hearing loss and dispense hearing aids.

Audiologists

Audiologists have a minimum of a master's degree in the evaluation and nonmedical treatment of hearing loss. Forty-seven states regulate the practice of audiology, and many audiologists are certified by the American Speech-Language-Hearing Association (ASHA). Most audiologists also fit and dispense hearing aids. The audiologist can determine the type and degree of hearing loss and whether or not you can be helped by a hearing aid (or aids), and if so, what type of hearing aid would be best for you.

Hearing Aid Specialists

Hearing aid specialists, also called hearing aid dealers, are licensed in all but four states to test hearing and sell hearing aids. While these dealers have less formal education and do not provide diagnostic audiological services, some have considerable experience. In many areas, hearing aid specialists are the only hearing health care specialists available.

MAKE SURE that whomever you choose is someone who spends adequate time informing and counseling you and in whom you have confidence and trust.

In addition to consulting professionals, begin to educate yourself about hearing loss. Go to the library and read everything you can find about hearing loss. Talk to friends who have a hearing loss or know someone who does. Learn strategies for coping with hearing loss and use them. These may make a difference in your ability to understand what is being said even before you see a hearing health care specialist.

Self Help for Hard of Hearing People (SHHH) has 250 local chapters across the country. Monthly meetings provide an opportunity for participants to learn from one another about successful strategies for living with hearing loss. Meeting other people who have a hearing loss helps you realize that you are not alone. Peer support helps you learn about hearing loss and ways to live with it.

(12)

Understanding Your Hearing Evaluation

WHETHER YOU have had your hearing tested many times before or are preparing for your first evaluation, a hearing assessment can be confusing and even overwhelming. You receive so much new information that you may find it hard to process everything.

Understanding what happens during a hearing evaluation and how that information relates to your communication abilities makes it possible for you to be an informed and active participant in shaping your hearing health care. In addition, you will be better equipped to judge whether you are receiving top-of-the-line, appropriate, and ethical service.

A hearing health care provider (audiologist or hearing aid specialist) begins the evaluation by taking a case history. You are asked about your hearing loss, situations in which you find it difficult to hear, and what you are not hearing at all. Don't forget to tell the tester about any medications you take regularly, especially ones that might be ototoxic (capable of causing hearing loss).

The tester will perform a battery of tests to determine the existence and extent of your hearing loss and your understanding of speech. All audiometric tests should be performed in a soundproof booth. Only in rare cases, such as when patients are bedridden, should they be performed in homes or elsewhere.

The tester either places earphones over your ears or inserts earphone to send sounds or speech to one or both ears. It is important that both ears be tested individually since the degree of hearing loss for each may differ. The tester will instruct you to raise your hand or a finger or push a button when you hear a sound. Be as alert as possible. Your responses to the tones will be reflected in the settings in your hearing aids.

The Hearing Evaluation

A complete hearing evaluation includes most of the following tests. Don't be afraid to ask what the tests are measuring.

Pure-Tone Air Conduction

The tester measures your ability to hear different tones of sound (frequencies), measured in Hertz (Hz) and your ability to hear the loudness or intensity of these tones, measured in decibels (dB).

Pure-Tone Bone Conduction

In this test the tester sends sound directly to your inner ear. The results determine whether you have a conductive, sensorineural, or mixed hearing loss.

Speech Reception and Speech Discrimination

In addition to the pure-tone test, the evaluator adjusts the volume and frequency to test your understanding (discrimination). During the test, you will hear a list of nonsense syllables, one-syllable words, and simple sentences, and you will be asked to repeat them. If your discrimination is 70 percent, you cannot understand 30 percent of the words you hear. The greater your discrimination loss, the more difficulty you will have understanding in situations with background noise, in poor acoustical settings, and if you are at a distance from the speaker.

Threshold of Awareness, Comfort, and Discomfort

Using connected speech stimuli, the tester measures your thresholds of speech awareness, comfort, and discomfort. These measures indicate your range of hearing (soft to loud) and provide important information when fitting a hearing aid. For example, individuals with severe sensitivity to loud sounds would require adaptive signal processing or compression in their hearing aid.

Impedance Testing

Impedance testing measures the ability of your eardrum to reflect sound waves. Too much or too little pressure on the inner side of the eardrum makes the eardrum too stiff to conduct and reflect sounds properly. The tester puts a probe covered with a soundproof material into your outer ear canal and seals up the entrance of the ear. A transmitter in the probe aims sounds at the eardrum. A receiver in the probe measures the reflections while air pumped through the probe changes the pressure in the canal rapidly from high to low. Abnormalities in this test may indicate abnormal middle ear function (conductive loss) for which a medical referral is warranted.

The Audiogram

The tester records your test results on an audiogram and then should explain the audiogram and its implications. At the beginning of your hearing evaluation, be sure to ask for a copy of your audiogram for your records. It is one of the first steps in understanding your hearing loss.

The audiogram will give you a basic picture of your ability to detect tones. The tester plots your hearing threshold—the very softest sound you can detect at a particular frequency—on a grid, with frequency (Hz) on the horizontal axis and loudness level (dB) on the vertical axis. Circles are used to record the threshold for your right ear and Xs indicate the left-ear thresholds. The degree of hearing loss is determined by the loudness level at which you can just detect sound (see figure 3).

Generally, Hz measurements start at 125 and increase in octave intervals up to 8,000 Hz. Loudness is measured in

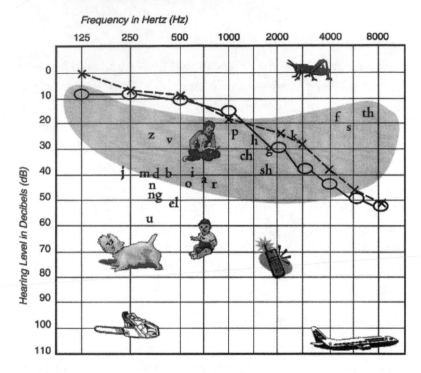

Figure 3. The audiogram is a graph that depicts hearing thresholds for selected tones (Hz) at various intensities (dB). The circles make the lowest intensity at which the right ear picks up tones, while the Xs show the thresholds for the left ear. The shaded area indicates the tones and intensities that individuals generally need to hear in order to recognize parts of speech clearly. The letters show the Hz and dB levels where individual speech sounds are heard, and the pictographs show the range of some common sounds. On an audiogram provided by your hearing health provider, the Xs and the circles are usually depicted in different colors for clarity.

10 dB increments, starting at 0 dB at the top of the audiogram and progressing to 110+ dB.

Whether or not you are an appropriate hearing aid candidate is determined by the combination of your hearing test results and your current communication needs. If hearing aids are recommended, be sure to ask about the various models, especially whether they contain options such as a telecoil and directional microphones, how they differ in function and in price, how they will help you, what their limitations are, and how to buy them.

(13)

Choosing a Hearing Aid Dispenser

IF YOUR hearing evaluation determines that amplification will help you hear better, you will have the important job of selecting a hearing aid dispenser. This person might be your audiologist or a licensed hearing aid dealer. This step is extremely important since you are choosing a person with whom you will have a long-term relationship, and, as in all relationships, you will want this to be comfortable, trusting, and mutually beneficial.

One way to find a responsive dispenser is to talk to friends and relatives who wear hearing aids, are comfortable with them, and have had a positive experience during the selection, purchase, and aural rehabilitation program. Selecting the right hearing aid takes time and patience. Not only will you have several visits with your hearing aid dispenser before the final purchase, you will return again and again for evaluations, repairs, education, and, eventually, new hearing aids.

You should expect the following skills, attitudes, and services from the hearing aid dispenser:

1. Interpersonal skills. Look for a person who is courteous and patient and willing to listen to you. The dispenser should see you as a person with a hearing loss, but one that has an individual lifestyle.
2. Competency. Be sure that the dispenser is licensed or certified, keeps up with the latest advances in hearing aids and fitting, and makes excellent earmold impressions.
3. Adequate diagnostic and testing equipment. The dispenser should perform tests in a soundproof room, have up-to-date testing equipment, and should provide you with an explanation of the results as well as a copy of your audiogram.
4. Selection assistance. The dispenser should explain clearly the difference in hearing aids and their performance and have a variety of brands and styles for you to try out in different communication situations, such as on the telephone, in a noisy location, and in your car. The dispenser also should provide information about options beyond the hearing aid, including assistive devices.
5. Education and rehabilitation services. The dispenser should describe how the aid functions as well as its limitations. When you receive your hearing aid, the dispenser should conduct a training session and follow up at periodic intervals to ensure your satisfaction. Some dispensers provide group hearing aid evaluation orientation sessions and evaluation for hearing assistive technology. If your dispenser does not offer an aural rehabilitation program, ask him or her to consider it or provide help in finding one.
6. Pricing and service policies. The dispenser should clearly explain all the costs that you can expect and which fees are nonrefundable if you need to return the

aid. Typically, costs for testing, custom-fit parts, and earmolds, are nonrefundable. You should expect to have at least a thirty-day (preferably sixty-day) trial period to try out the aid (this is the law in some states). This gives you time to "test-drive" the aid, just as you would when buying a new car. The dispenser should provide repair service and give you a loaner free of charge should your aid need repair (see chapter 17).

7. Parking facilities and proximity to public transportation. A dispenser whose facility is located near public transportation or has convenient parking may be a consideration for some older people.

HEARING AIDS are expensive. Don't be rushed into a decision. Choose a dispenser whose primary goal is to satisfy your needs.

(14)

Will a Hearing Aid Help?

A HEARING aid will not correct or restore your hearing, but it will help you to hear by amplifying sounds. Most hearing aids have a manual volume control that allows you to increase or decrease the volume as needed. Some newer models have a built-in volume control (automatic signal processing) that does this automatically.

A hearing aid will amplify all the sounds in your environment. Sometimes this is desirable since you want to hear the telephone and doorbell as well as other sounds that alert you to changes; however, hearing aids also will amplify dinnerware clanging and background noise in large group settings.

If you have trouble hearing and differentiating between certain sounds such as f and s (high-frequency sounds), your hearing aid can be set to increase the volume of those sounds, which can influence the clarity and help you hear better.

If you have difficulty hearing on the telephone, a hearing aid with a T-switch (telecoil) will enable you to hear on the telephone and use a variety of assistive technologies to improve your telephone communications (see chapters 18 and 20).

There are many manufacturers and many models of hearing aids and there are new models coming on the market every year. There is no "best" hearing aid. Each person has an individualized hearing loss; what is right for others may not be right for you. Just because someone you know is happy with his or her aid does not mean that it will work well for you. Hearing aid selection depends on many factors, including the degree of your hearing loss, your demands on hearing, your manual dexterity, the situations in which you communicate, and how much you can afford to spend.

Hearing aids are not comparable to eyeglasses, which can correct vision to normal. In fact, the sounds coming through the hearing aid can at first sound unnatural—tinny and mechanical. With continued use, the auditory system adapts to this new sound and it is then perceived to be more like "normal" sound. Many people who expect "normal" hearing through a new hearing aid are disappointed and, after a few brief trials, stick the aid in a bureau drawer permanently.

A first-time hearing aid user may be disturbed or distracted by some everyday sounds, such as footsteps, birds chirping, and paper shuffling, especially when these sounds have not been heard in years. With time and use of the hearing aid, the sounds become less disturbing and even enjoyable. However, when hearing aids are optimally fit, the brain can reorganize new sound patterns, which permits you to have increased sound perception. New hearing aid users need at least a six- to eight-week adjustment period to determine the full benefit.

Properly selected, properly fitted, and properly used with follow-up care, a hearing aid is a positive start to dealing with your hearing loss. The initial steps of coming to terms with not hearing well and getting a hearing aid need not be overwhelming. Many successful hearing aid users will tell you that a hearing aid has brought them out of isolation and greatly increased their independence and quality of life.

(15)

Types of Hearing Aids

ALL HEARING aids work in a similar fashion and have similar parts. These include the following:

- a microphone to pick up sound
- an amplifier to make sound louder
- a receiver (miniature loudspeaker) to deliver the louder sound to the ear
- batteries to power the electronic parts

Some hearing aids also have earmolds to channel the flow of sound into the ear, enhance sound quality, and help hold the hearing aid in place. Other hearing aids are built right into the earmold casing.

Hearing aids also differ in design, circuitry (analog and digital), power, ease of handling, and availability of special features such as telecoils and directional microphones. You, in consultation with your hearing aid dispenser, should decide which of the many styles and options best meets your needs.

Types of Hearing Aids in Use Today

Behind-the-Ear

Behind-the-ear (BTE) hearing aids fit securely behind the ear and are coupled to a custom-made earmold. BTEs are suitable for the entire range of hearing losses. These models can include a telecoil.

In-the-Ear

In-the-ear (ITE) hearing aids fit into the contour of the outer ear with a portion extending into the ear canal. They are larger and more visible than canal aids and can be used by people with hearing losses ranging from mild to moderately-severe. These models can also include a telecoil.

In-the-Canal

In-the-canal (ITC) hearing aids are contained in a tiny case that fits into the ear canal. If your hearing loss is mild and you hear well on the telephone, you may want to consider this model. However, if you have trouble with manual dexterity, consider a different model. These aids usually do not include a telecoil or a volume control. Sound level is automatic.

Completely-in-the-Canal

Completely-in-the-canal (CIC) hearing aids are growing in popularity because of their cosmetic appeal and the fact that they can be fit to a broad range of hearing losses (mild to severe). Nearly all of the CICs currently dispensed are programmable or digital.

CROS and BICROS

CROS (Contralateral Routing of Signal) and BICROS (Bilateral Routing of Signals) are instruments designed to transmit sound from a microphone located near a nonfunctional or unaidable ear to a receiver on the other ear. A CROS aid is used if the better ear has close to normal hearing; a BICROS aid is used if both ears require amplification.

Body-Worn

Body-worn hearing aids are large and very powerful aids that are used for profound hearing losses. The microphone and amplifiers are contained in a case that is worn on the body (clipped to the inside of a blouse or pocket); a cord connecting the case to the receiver runs along the neck; and the receiver then snaps into an earmold with wires extending from the receiver. Very few people now wear body aids.

Programmable and Digital

The latest generation of hearing aids, programmable and digital hearing aids, are extremely sophisticated electronic devices. Some that are on the market are essentially minicomputers. They can be programmed to provide different kinds of amplification characteristics depending on your hearing loss, with some including a multiple-memory mode that can be modified as the listening situation changes. These hearing aids tend to be much more expensive than more conventional hearing aids and the cost-benefit ratio may not be sufficient to justify the extra expense. For this reason, it is important to have confidence in the skills and advice of your hearing aid dispenser and have the option to return the hearing aid(s) after a trial period.

The newest entry on the hearing aid scene is the digital hearing aid. In a digital hearing aid, the sound signals that are picked up by the microphone are converted to binary bits of information (hence the term *digital*). This type of conversion permits the sound to be manipulated in ways not possible with a purely analog hearing aid. Having met the technical challenge to produce wearable digital hearing aids, the manufacturers are now busy trying to develop speech-processing strategies of proven value for listeners. The major question, however, is not "digital" versus "analog," but determining exactly what kind of amplification pattern the digital hearing aid should provide a specific listener.

Many people can be helped equally as well with an advanced analog hearing aid as with a digital aid; others, for whom a particular digital aid may offer unique advantages should personally determine whether the perceived benefits of the digital hearing aid justify the extra costs.

Disposable

Disposable hearing aids are targeted for people with mild to moderate hearing loss and who are not hearing aid users. The aid is designed to last for forty days when used twelve hours a day. The dispenser selects one of nine different programs to match the configuration of the person with hearing loss. Because the device is discarded when the battery runs out, there is no need for a battery door, freeing that space for a larger than usual microphone.

Implantable

Implantable hearing aids are designed to deliver sound directly to one of the middle ear bones (the incus). The aid consists of two portions. An internal portion is surgically implanted behind the ear in much the same way as a cochlear implant (see chapter 21). A wire from this unit terminates in a small "oscillator" that is crimped on one of the middle ear bones. The external portion contains the microphone and other hearing aid circuitry and it is joined to the internal portion via magnetic attraction. These hearing aids are of particular benefit for people who are unable to wear an earmold in their ear canal for some reason (allergy, chronic infections, etc.) or who are unable to tolerate their own voice when an earmold is inserted in their ear canals.

Bone Anchored

Bone anchored hearing aids (BAHA) are for patients with a conductive hearing loss and for some patients with a mixed loss. Typical candidates are people with irresolvable middle ear dysfunction that has not responded to medical or surgical intervention, or congenital facio-cranial conditions. A titanium screw is implanted in the mastoid process behind the ear. When vibrated by a special hearing aid connected to the screw, bone conduction vibrations are transmitted through the skull directly to the cochlea.

Binaural

If you have a loss in both ears, your audiologist should recommend that you consider a binaural fitting (two hearing aids). There are many advantages to wearing two aids, including improved listening in noisy environments and determining from which direction a sound is coming. As is always the case with a hearing aid purchase, be sure you can return one aid at the end of the trial period if you are uncomfortable or unsuccessful wearing two aids.

Hearing Aid Special Features

Several options to consider when selecting a hearing aid follow.

T-Switch or Telecoil

Some hearing aids have a switch that allows you to select microphone (M) or telecoil (T). Some aids also have a combination M-T-switch, which activates the telecoil and microphone simultaneously. Hearing aids incorporating a T-switch are often no more expensive if you request the switch at the time of testing or purchase. The T-switch is an option that can be included in all but the tiniest aids (CICs). This feature is important for several reasons. It allows you to hear without getting feedback when using the telephone or assistive listening devices. It also allows you to focus on hearing speech in noisy situations.

Direct Audio Input

Many models of behind-the-ear hearing aids are designed to accept direct audio input. An adapter shoe or boot connects the hearing aid receiver to an assistive listening device, TV, stereo, or Walkman or to an external microphone via wire cords. This connection bypasses the hearing aid's microphone and can dramatically improve the signal-to-noise ratio (hearing speech over noise). Some BTE and most CIC, ITC, and ITE aids do not accept direct audio input.

Directional Microphones

A feature that has been proven of value in hearing aids is the directional microphone. They are especially beneficial in difficult listening situations, such as group settings. The directional microphone picks up critical speech signals delivered in front of the hearing aid user while reducing the amount of amplification from the rear and sides.

Ear-Level Personal FM Receiver

This FM receiver can fit into a behind-the-ear style hearing aid case and can be used either as a hearing aid or as an FM receiver. Other FM receivers are integrated in an audio adapter that clips on to the hearing aid and can remain locked in place or removed again in seconds. An advantage to these receivers is that there is no body-worn receiver.

(16)

The Importance of Fitting Hearing Aids

WHEN THE testing and evaluation of your hearing determines that you can benefit from a hearing aid, the hearing aid dispenser will proceed with the proper fitting.

Making an Impression

The hearing aid dispenser will insert a soft waxlike material into your ear to make an impression of your ear canal and outer ear. This is an essential part of the hearing aid fitting. If you decide to purchase an in-the-ear (ITE) or in-the-canal (ITC) aid, this step is extremely important because, if not done properly, the aid will not fit correctly. If you decide to purchase a behind-the-ear (BTE) aid, you also will need an impression in order to have an earmold made.

Earmolds

The purpose of the earmold is to couple the sound from your hearing aid to your ear. The degree and configuration of your hearing loss determines the type of earmold you need. There are many different kinds of earmolds and it is important to have the kind that is right for you. The hearing aid dispenser will send the impression to a laboratory where it is copied in a hard (acrylic) or soft (polyvinyl) synthetic material. Non-allergenic polyethylene is recommended for people who have allergic reactions to the other two materials.

When the earmold is returned from the manufacturer, the dispenser will ensure that the fit is tight so that all amplified sound goes into your ear. An earmold that is too small causes feedback (whistling or squealing), or you may hear an echo when you speak, or the sound may be distorted. One that is too large will not fit or may be uncomfortable. Sometimes the dispenser can file it to fit; however, if that does not work, you should expect the impression and earmold to be remade at no additional cost.

If you consider trying a BTE, the hearing aid dispenser will connect the mold to several different BTE hearing aids and you can select the one that is best for you. The dispenser may try several models of one brand or several different brands before you both can decide which one helps you most in the environments where you will need it most.

If you decide to try an ITE or ITC, the impression taken for the mold is used to construct the hearing aid. This is why a good earmold impression is always essential.

Once you have selected a hearing aid, the dispenser will evaluate your hearing with the aid in place and measure the increased benefit you receive from the aid, keeping appropriate records so that you are always able to compare your current situation to a previous one.

Feedback

Feedback occurs when some of the amplified sound escapes from around the earmold or the ITE or ITC aid, gets picked up by the hearing aid microphone, and then is reamplified to start the process all over again. Some feedback is normal, such as when you cup your hand over your ear, if you remove your aid without turning it off, or if you lie down with your aid turned on. However, if you get feedback when you chew or smile, or when you turn the volume higher, it may be a sign that the mold or aid does not fit well.

Replacing the Mold

Since the ear is made of cartilage, it is always changing in shape and size. At the same time, vinyl materials tend to shrink over time. You, therefore, should have your mold checked regularly to determine if you need a new one. If the mold has become discolored or hard, it's time to get a new one.

Cleaning the Earmold

Each evening, when you remove your hearing aid, you should wipe the earmold with a tissue. If you have a problem with earwax clogging the mold, this step is even more important because the smallest amount of wax can affect the sound reception. If the earmold can be removed from the aid, you can soak it in warm dishwashing liquid and water once a week. Dry it carefully before attaching it to the aid. A small rubber ball syringe will remove the moisture from the tubing. Do not use alcohol or other chemicals to clean your earmold since they may cause it to crack. Nonallergenic material may need to be washed more often, as it tends to grip in the ear canal, sponging up earwax and dirt.

Wax

Earwax or *cerumen* is the body's natural way of lubricating the ear canal and keeping insects out of it since they do not like the odor; however, wax may obstruct the canal so that sound does not pass through clearly. For that reason it is important to have a doctor remove the wax from your ear canals before you are evaluated for a hearing loss. Wax also can clog earmold openings or plug up vents in hearing aids, so these should be checked daily. You can clean small amounts of wax from the earmold or tubing with a pipe cleaner or the tool provided by the hearing aid manufacturer.

(17)

Purchasing a Hearing Aid

Where to Begin

SELECTING THE right hearing aid for purchase is an important decision. It also can be stressful, especially if it is your first hearing aid. With other important purchases, such as auto-mobiles and refrigerators, we can depend on recommendations from friends who have had good experiences with those products. But since each person's hearing loss is individualized, the make and model of a hearing aid that works well for your friend may not be beneficial to you. You need to choose the aid that works best for *you*.

Be an Educated Consumer

Becoming an educated consumer is key to your success in choosing the right hearing aid. Your hearing aid dispenser should point out the pros and cons of various aids in terms of ease of handling, comfort, and suitability based on your hearing loss. You, in turn, must state your specific needs.

Do you have difficulty hearing on the telephone? In one-on-one conversations? In restaurants? In places of worship? At the movies? At meetings? You need to communicate all of this to your hearing aid dispenser. The final choice should emerge from your responses while trying out several makes and models and considering the advantages and disadvantages of each.

Although hearing aids last for four or more years, they are expensive. They range in price from $750 to $3,000. Many hearing aid dispensers include testing, fitting, and follow-up visits in the price of the hearing aid, while others do not. When testing fees are separate, the hearing aid should cost less. Find out what services the cost includes. The average price for hearing aids follows:

Digital aid	$3,000
Programmable aid	$1,563
In-the-canal aid	$ 952
In-the-ear aid	$ 762
Behind-the-ear aid	$ 750

The newest generation of programmable digital hearing aids may cost as much as $3,000. These prices in most instances include testing and fitting.

Ask your hearing aid dispenser about options available in the hearing aid such as a T-switch or direct audio input (see chapter 15). These cost less when included at the time of purchase as opposed to adding them later.

The Sales Contract

When you purchase a hearing aid, be sure to get a purchase agreement or sales contract containing all the terms of the transaction in writing, and read it carefully. It should include the following items:

Price

Prices vary depending on the kind and model, where you purchase the aid, and what services are provided. This is one good reason to ask what the price includes.

Payment Agreement

Your contract should explain the payment terms in detail, including such items as down payment, interest, other charges, and insurance coverage.

Trial Period

The normal trial period for a hearing aid is thirty days. During this period, you may return the aid for any reason, provided it is in good condition. The trial period should be explained up front. Be sure you know whether thirty days means calendar or working days. If you are offered or can negotiate a longer trial period, by all means do so because it takes some time for the brain to adjust to the new sounds you will be hearing.

What Is Refundable?

If you decide to return the aid, you may have to pay a user's fee for the thirty-day trial period. If you decide to purchase the aid, the fee is waived. If you return a behind-the-ear hearing aid, you will be charged a fee for making the ear-mold. This fee is nonrefundable; however, the earmolds are yours to keep. Dispensing audiologists have different fee structures, so it is important to find out up front what is refundable.

Rehabilitation Services

Most new users need training and help adjusting to hearing aids. You may need two or three visits after you get your new aid to ensure that you understand its potential and are getting maximum benefit. With the newer programmable and digital aids, you may need even more visits. If your hearing health care specialist offers group rehabilitation sessions, be sure to enroll. Learning to be a successful hearing aid user requires practice. This service is an important part of your contract.

Warranty

Almost all hearing aids carry a one- or two-year warranty for defects in material or workmanship. Most warranties do not cover external receivers, cords, earmolds, tubing, or batteries. Some offer a one-year loss and damage policy. Read over the warranty and inquire whether it is honored by the dispenser, the manufacturer, or both. You may wish to mark your calendar on a date several weeks before the warranty expires to remind you to be sure that the aid is in good working order. Inquire whether additional insurance coverage against damage or loss and extended warranties are available at the time of purchase.

Third-Party Providers

Your health care plan, Medicare, or Medicaid may cover costs for a hearing test and hearing aid evaluation, but very few health insurance policies cover the cost of hearing aids. Medicare doesn't cover them at all. Medicaid, which is restricted to eligible participants, provides for one aid only with upper limits on the cost.

Other Costs to Consider

Consider the following costs when purchasing an aid.

Batteries

Different aids use different sizes and types of batteries. Find out which batteries are used in your model, how long they last, and how much they cost. The length of time batteries last depends on how much you use the aid and at what power/volume setting.

Repairs

Hearing aids sometimes need to be repaired. If your hearing aid malfunctions, it is best to take it to the dispenser for proper diagnosis and advice. Sometimes the dispenser may be able to fix the aid "in-house" at less cost to you. Major repairs may take longer because the aid needs to be sent back to the manufacturer. Your dispenser may offer you a loaner. When the warranty and service plan expire, you will need to pay for repairs. The cost of the repair service (out of warranty) usually includes a three- or six-month repair warranty.

Other Options for Payment

Many civic and service organizations recondition hearing aids and put them in the hands of people who need them.

Speech and hearing centers may provide hearing aids at a reduced rate for their clients. Hear Now provides aids to people who need them and also welcomes donations of used hearing aids (see appendix A). All World War I veterans are eligible to receive free hearing aids. The eligibility of other veterans is decided on a case by case basis. Vocational Rehabilitation provides services for clients who meet eligibility requirements.

A Word of Caution

Never purchase a hearing aid by mail or by phone. Remember that you are not only purchasing a device but also the services of a specialist who will test the fit and fine tune the aid when needed. This is a dispenser with whom you have developed a good working relationship and who will advise you over the course of the service.

(18)

When Hearing Aids Are Not Enough

WHILE HEARING aids are beneficial to many people, they may need to be supplemented in some situations. Even with hearing aids, people with hearing loss may have a great deal of difficulty understanding speech in noisy situations or when the sound source is some distance from them.

If you are unable to hear well at ceremonies relating to celebrations of life—such as weddings, baptisms, bar mitzvahs, and funerals—your hearing loss may be creating a barrier that could result in a deep sense of deprivation and loss. If you are reluctant to participate in community and congregational life because you cannot hear well, you may be needlessly isolating yourself from activities. Nevertheless, if the meeting and lecture rooms you frequent are not equipped with a public address (PA) or an assistive listening system (ALS), thus making dialogue inaccessible to you, don't give up.

In recent years, the development of assistive technology designed to supplement hearing aids has burgeoned. New devices are developed, improved, and marketed each year. Three general types have been developed: assistive listening devices (ALDs), various kinds of signaling and warning devices (see chapter 19), and telecommunication devices (see chapter 20).

Assistive Listening Systems

Assistive listening systems can help you hear better at home and in public situations ranging from movies to business meetings to large group gatherings. All assistive listening systems enhance hearing in everyday situations by reducing the negative effects of distance, background noise, and reverberations. They do this by transmitting sound picked up by a microphone or via a direct connection to an audio source, such as a movie sound track, television, stereo, and telephone, directly to the ears of a listener. A magnetic field, radio wave, or infrared light beam transmits the sound directly to the ears of the person with a hearing loss via a special receiver. All systems are wireless and work well with or without hearing aids. All systems come in personal and large-area versions. All work effectively when appropriately selected and installed. Choosing the right assistive listening system requires careful thought. The best way to choose an ALS is to assess your needs, discuss them with a professional, and try out the systems available.

Large-Area Assistive Listening Systems

If you have a mild hearing loss, a good PA system may be sufficient. If your loss is more severe, an assistive listening system can be combined with the PA system in order to feed the sound directly into your ear.

Large-area assistive listening systems are effective for enhancing listening in large rooms of assembly, places of worship, museums, theaters and movies, convention centers, public agency meeting rooms, and corporate conference rooms. Three types of large-area listening systems are now in use: audio induction loop (magnetic waves), infrared (light waves), and FM (radio waves).

All of the systems have a microphone that takes in sound, a transmitter that will send sound signals across a distance, a receiver to convert the sound signals, and a coupler to transmit sound to a listener's ear. All systems have volume control settings that can be adjusted by the individual user, can help to minimize the effects of poor acoustic condition in the room, and can be used with public address systems.

Audio Induction Loop System

The audio induction loop is a coil of electrical wire that is placed around a selected area (see figure 4). The wire, which creates a magnetic field that can transmit sound, is connected to an amplifier and to the speaker's microphone, TV, tape recorder, or other sound source. It differs from a public address system in that the amplified signal is sent to the coil of wire rather than to the loudspeakers. The magnetic field

Figure 4. Audio induction loop system

around the wire is picked up by individuals who wear hearing aids equipped with a telecoil (T-switch). The signal also can be picked up with a headset and receiver if the hard of hearing person is not wearing a hearing aid. The hard of hearing person can sit anywhere inside or alongside the loop and hear the sound without the disturbing effects of background noise or echoes. The PA system and audio induction loop should be used together because people with hearing loss listen in different ways. Loops, usually permanently installed in a room, also come in portable versions.

Infrared System

This system is often found in theaters, courtrooms, and other public facilities. The transmission is similar to using a remote control with a television set. The signal is sent out in a sixty-degree cone like the beam from a flashlight. The hard of hear-

Figure 5. Infrared system

ing person who does not wear hearing aids wears a headset with a receiver that picks up sound from the infrared light beam. Listeners who wear hearing aids with a T-switch can wear a neck loop plugged into the receiver with a photosensitive diode (see figure 5); listeners whose hearing aid does not have a T-switch can use a silhouette behind the ear plugged into the receiver. Infrared is the choice when privacy is essential. Because light does not transmit through walls, several systems can be used in a building. An infrared system can be used outdoors if strong sunlight is not shining directly on the diodes of the emitter.

FM (Frequency Modulation) System

The Federal Communications Commission has designated certain radio frequencies for use by people with hearing loss. FM systems can be used for listening in large areas, such as classrooms, auditoriums, movie houses, and places of worship—the kinds of places where hard of hearing people typically have a great deal of difficulty understanding speech.

Figure 6. FM system

A "large-area" FM transmitter can be hooked into an existing PA system. The hard of hearing person who does not wear hearing aids wears a headset with a receiver that picks up sound. Listeners who wear hearing aids with a T-switch can wear a neck loop plugged into an FM receiver; listeners whose hearing aid does not have a T-switch can use a silhouette behind the ear plugged into the receiver (see figure 6). FM works extremely well in delivering a clear speech signal to hard of hearing people in these stressful listening conditions. FM systems can transmit through walls and buildings. Therefore, multiple frequencies are required for adjacent room usage.

Personal Listening Systems

Personal listening systems are commonly called "hard-wired" systems. Instead of transmitting signals across great distances through the aid, these systems transmit signals across much shorter distances through a connecting wire.

One-on-One Communicators

These acoustic amplifiers include a built-in microphone and an amplifier and can accommodate most types of headphones. They are particularly helpful in small group situations when background noise interferes with your ability to understand the speaker. You may find these helpful in restaurants, at small group meetings, and in the car when you and the driver wish to keep your eyes on the road.

Personal FM Systems

Personal FM systems can be used to help in any situation where it is possible to place the microphone close to the sound source, such as in a noisy restaurant, moving car, small meetings, and near a TV loudspeaker. Personal FM systems can be used for tours, lectures, in the car, and small group conversations. They are particularly helpful when talking to one other person in noisy situations such as parties, restaurants, and meetings. The speaker uses a microphone connected to a small FM transmitter while the hard of hearing person uses an FM receiver connected to earphones or personal hearing aids. The transmitter and the receiver need to be set to the same radio frequency.

Television Listening Devices

Television has become our window on the world; when we cannot hear and understand TV, we are frustrated. When we turn the volume up in order to hear what is amplified through the loudspeakers, the noise can be disturbing to others. Several TV listening devices (loops, FM, infrared) are available to

enable a person who is hard of hearing to hear without turning the volume too loud for other listeners. The principle is the
same as with large-area listening systems: The sound is picked
up from the TV set (by placing a microphone close to the loudspeaker or by plugging the listening device into an audio
output jack). The TV sound is then transmitted directly to the
ears of the person wearing the hearing device.

Closed Captions

In addition to TV listening devices, you may want to consider captions if you are having difficulty understanding
what is being said on television. Closed captions are the text
display of spoken dialogue and sounds that are visible with
the use of a decoder. All new TV sets thirteen inches or larger
come with built-in closed caption chips that can be activated
to show captions when desired. The built-in chip requirement also applies to digital TVs with displays that are at least
7.8 inches vertically. Older TV sets can be connected to separate telecaption decoders, which operate to present the same
closed-caption message. Nearly all prime-time television
programming for major networks is closed captioned.

Other Assistive Visual Systems

Listed below are several visual systems that allow people
with hearing loss to attend and participate in classes, meetings, and other group settings.

CART

Communication access realtime translation (CART) is the
instant conversion of the spoken word into English text,
using a stenotype machine, notebook computer, and realtime
software, to facilitate full participation by people with hear-

ing loss. With this technology, the message can be displayed on a video monitor, printed out as a rough transcript, captured on a floppy disk or CD, or printed in Braille seconds after information is transmitted by the CART reporter to the computer. This system is a verbatim system.

C-Print

This computer-aided speech-to-print transcription system provides a "near verbatim" readout. Using word processing software aided by abbreviation software, the trained captionist condenses the speaker's words into a laptop computer. The typed information is displayed simultaneously on a second laptop, television monitor, or screen. Although not as exact as CART, C-print is more complete than computer-assisted notetaking (CAN).

CAN

Computer-assisted notetaking is best done by a fast, accurate typist who can summarize materials well. Using a computer keyboard, the typist takes notes, which are then displayed visually on a screen or laptop monitor.

ASR

Automatic Speech Recognition (ASR), currently in the developmental stages, recognizes and converts the spoken word into text. The speaker speaks into a special microphone clearly and evenly at a conversational pace. ASR offers new alternatives for providing communication access in the future.

(19)

Hearing the Doorbell, Telephone, and Fire Alarm

YOU MAY find that you have difficulty hearing a ringing doorbell or telephone, a knock on the door, a smoke or fire alarm, an alarm clock, a baby's cry, and other sounds that alert people to daily life occurrences. Fortunately, signaling devices are available to help compensate for your hearing loss and allow you to gain a greater sense of confidence and security at home, on the job, and while traveling.

Signaling Devices

The principle of all signaling devices is to detect sound by producing visual signals or vibrations that supplement auditory signals. If you have a mild hearing loss, however, increasing the volume (e.g., a loud telephone extension ringer) may enhance hearing. If your hearing loss is severe you may find signaling equipment helpful. The most common signaling device is a flashing light, but you may prefer a vibrating device placed under your pillow or mattress or under the cushion of your chair. Inexpensive systems are limited to one designated sound, but sophisticated systems are available that incorporate light patterns for various sounds.

Wake-Up Devices

If you cannot hear the alarm on your clock, you may want to consider one of the many alerting devices on the market. If you are easily awakened by light, you may prefer a clock that flashes your bedside lamp. If you are a deep sleeper, consider a vibrating unit that can be placed under the pillow or mattress. If a gentle breeze is sufficient to wake you up, consider an electric fan connected to the clock. If you have a mild hearing loss, consider a clock with an enhanced audible alarm. Some clocks provide all of the options. Many of these devices are battery operated and portable.

Timers

When you are awake, there are times when you need to be alerted such as when a meal is finished cooking or when your have a few minutes left to complete a task. The devices mentioned above will serve the purpose.

Smoke or Fire Alarms

If you are concerned about being able to hear the alarm from your smoke detector, you may want to purchase a smoke detector that combines a built-in horn and a strobe light. Others have a separate horn that plugs into an electrical outlet in the bedroom or elsewhere in the house. A lamp, strobe, or vibrating device also can plug into a portable receiver. The system should be set up in such a way that the sensor is located where the smoke might be likely to occur and the alerting component installed where you are likely to be (for example, in the bedroom). Shop wisely since only a few brands are recommended by the National Fire Protection Association.

Hearing the Telephone and the Doorbell

If you have turned up the telephone ringer volume as high as possible and still can't hear it when the water is running or the television is on, consider a loud tone ringer, a light flasher, or vibrating alert. If you cannot hear the doorbell ring when you are a distance from its source, consider placing a ringer in the room you are in most frequently or connecting it to an alerting device.

Paging Systems

Battery-powered receivers worn on the wrist or the waist can keep you in touch with family and friends. Pagers can receive messages from touch-tone phones, personal computers, and TTYs.* Vibrating pagers with alphanumeric display screens offer a new way to contact hard of hearing people. You also may want to consider a personal pager that uses a radio system to alert people in close proximity that it is time for dinner or that they are needed in another part of the house. This is especially helpful for invalids and caregivers.

In the Car

If you are not able to hear your turn signal when driving, consider a visual device that alerts you when the turn signal has been on for an extraordinary length of time. Several automobile companies offer a rebate for the complete cost of this device and installation on recently purchased or leased vehicles.

Purchasing Signaling Devices

The number of signaling and alerting devices on the market grows daily and making a decision about the best one to buy is not easy. Your audiologist can provide guidance. Visit a hearing rehabilitation center if one is located near you. Talk

---

*TTYs are telecommunication devices that allow deaf and hard of hearing people to converse over telephone lines.

to other hard of hearing people who have purchased devices and have found them helpful. The best place to try out a variety of devices is at the annual convention of Self Help for Hard of Hearing People (SHHH). For a list of the several demonstration centers in the United States, contact SHHH (see chapter 41).

Hearing Dogs

Hearing dogs are trained by professionals as service dogs to alert their owners to various significant sounds. When one of these sounds occurs, the dog attracts the owner's attention and leads him or her to the sound. In the case of a fire alarm, the dog attracts the owner's attention and then drops to the ground. Hearing dogs may be any breed or mixed breed. They are working animals and can be reliable protectors and loving, loyal companions. Like all dogs, they must be fed, kept clean, walked, and loved. Hearing dogs are permitted in all public places just as are guide and other service dogs for people with vision loss and other disabilities. If you live alone, you may wish to consider owning a hearing dog (see appendix A).

(20)

Hearing on the Telephone

SO MUCH of our life revolves around using the telephone—it is our connection with the world. We use it to make appointments, chat with family and friends, and call for help in an emergency. We need to use the telephone if we are in the work force and also if we are community volunteers. Good telephone communication has long been a requirement for hard of hearing individuals.

Some people with hearing loss hear well on the telephone, but many people with hearing loss need to have the sound amplified moderately. Others need to use a hearing aid with a telecoil (T-switch) to receive the message clearly, while still others may need to use a TTY or other telephone device.

The T-Switch

The T-switch, variously known as the telecoil, the induction coil, and the induction pick-up coil, is a special feature on a hearing aid that uses the principle of inductive coupling. The T-switch has many uses besides telephone communication since it can link the hearing aid to other sources of magnetic energy, the most common of which are the audioloop system and a host of assistive listening devices (see chapter 18).

Hard of hearing people have found that hearing aids with telecoils can be used with much success on telephones that are hearing-aid compatible. Flipping a small switch from the normal setting to the "T" setting when using a hearing aid on the telephone not only reduces the sound of background noise and eliminates feedback that sometimes occurs when your hearing aid is set on microphone position but also makes it easier to concentrate on the conversation. If your hearing aid does not have a telecoil, you may want to explore having a telecoil added or consider an aid with a telecoil when you purchase a new one.

Telephone Devices

You may wish to investigate the many telephone listening devices on the market that meet the varying needs of hard of hearing people. Some people find older, reconditioned telephones provide the best reception.

Choosing the right telephone device depends on your needs and the environment in which you will use it. Before buying any device, try different kinds of equipment. Ask other people with hearing loss about their experience with the product. Each device has advantages and disadvantages. Consider your needs along with the cost of the device.

Amplified Telephones

Telephones can be amplified by using a handset with a volume control built in, a portable amplifier that slips onto the handset, an in-line amplifier attached to a regular phone, or a phone with built-in amplification. Cordless phones also have models that provide amplification. Amplifiers can be used with or without a hearing aid.

1. **Built-in amplifiers**. If you regularly use the same telephone, you can replace the standard handset with one that has a built-in amplifier. The volume control allows you to set the volume at a comfortable level and also allows you to adjust the volume for different voices. Other people using the same handset can adjust the level to the normal volume. When replacing the standard handset with an amplified one, be sure it will function with the brand and model of the telephone. Other telephones allow you to enhance speech sounds by pressing amplify buttons or sliding a control bar in order to increase the volume. The most common models can provide 20dB of gain, which may be all that is needed for telephone communication for people with mild hearing loss; however, several brands offer models with much higher volume, a good reason for choosing an amplified telephone.

2. **Portable amplifiers.** These are convenient when traveling or if you use several different telephones. With this
   device, the battery-powered amplifier slips over the
   handset earpiece, and you can adjust the volume to suit
   your needs. Although easy to attach and operate, the
   portable amplifier may not work on all telephones or
   make the volume as loud as some hard of hearing people
   need it to be.
3. **In-line amplifiers.** These are connected between the
   base of the telephone and the standard handset cord, and
   are best for a permanent placement. The device allows
   you to adjust the volume as needed. Before you buy one,
   make sure it will function with the brand and model of
   the telephone to which you intend to connect it.

TTYs (Text Telephone)

If you find that neither amplification nor the T-switch allows
you to communicate well on the telephone, you should consider a TTY, formerly called a TT or TDD. TTYs make it possible for hard of hearing people who cannot use an amplified
telephone to communicate over a standard telephone. TTYs
allow you to see/read what someone is saying. You may
receive the message directly from another TTY or indirectly
via the relay service. Some TTYs are made up of a type-
writer-like keyboard, a telephone coupler, and some form of
visual display. Some TTYs have a direct connect option. The
visual display may be in the form of printed characters on
paper, an alphanumeric display on an LED screen, or both.
The latest models of TTYs have a voice carry-over (VCO)
mode so that the hard of hearing person can speak the message but receive the answer on the TTY. Some models are
portable providing users freedom and convenience by eas-

ily attaching to any phone. The emergency number 9-1-1 is TTY accessible.

Telecommunications Relay Service

Telecommunications Relay Service provides full telephone accessibility to people who are deaf, hard of hearing, deaf-blind, or speech disabled (see figure 7). Specially trained communication assistants (CAs) serve as intermediaries, relaying conversations between hearing people and people using a text telephone (TTY). Relay service is available twenty-four hours a day, 365 days a year, with no restrictions on the length or number of calls placed. This valuable communications tool gives all individuals the opportunity to make personal and business calls just like any other telephone user. This option not only serves people who are hard

Figure 7. Telecommunications Relay Service

of hearing but also those with speech disabilities. To use a relay service, you dial 7-1-1.

TTYs allow a hearing person to speak to a CA, who will in turn type the message to the person with the hearing loss. Conversely, the person with hearing loss can type to the CA who will relay the message orally to the hearing person. The CA, also called a relay operator, then types the spoken reply back via the TTY. You may want to use voice carry-over mode with the relay service as well. In a VCO call, you speak directly to the other party, whose voiced response is typed back to you by the relay operator. TTYs are often available free or at reduced rates through a state distribution program. Relay services are available in all fifty states for calls placed within the state and throughout the world.

Electronic Mail

The computer age has ushered in another popular way to communicate: e-mail. This service allows people with hearing loss to communicate easily with people they would ordinarily converse with on the telephone without the stress of listening. Chatting via instant messaging is another bonus for using e-mail.

Voice Messaging

Many people today use voice mail instead of a telephone answering machine. One advantage of voice mail is that you can use your preferred amplified phone to listen to voice mail messages. You can also retrieve the messages using the relay and read them on a TTY. The relay operator can also retrieve your messages and type them while you are on the line. There is a cost for voice mail but many people like it because callers can leave messages even when the line is in use. If you prefer to use an answering machine and have difficulty understanding the message, you may want to consider a machine with an audio output jack. When the jack is used, the internal loudspeaker is bypassed. Hard of hearing people can use the answering machine by either plugging in high-quality headphones or using a neck loop to inductively couple the output to the hearing aid telecoil.

Caller ID

Most telephone companies offer caller ID, which lets you see the name and number of the incoming call before you answer the telephone. Knowing who you are talking to before picking up the receiver often helps you get over the initial embarrassment of not getting a caller's name. You also can get caller ID displayed on your television screen.

Cellular Phones

Cellular telephones have become increasingly popular. Most of them have volume control and some have built-in hearing aid compatibility (HAC). If you purchase a cellular telephone, be sure you try different models to determine which sounds best and is easiest to use.

A new generation of cellular telephones, called digital wireless telephone, recently was introduced into some communities in the United States. These new phones have many advantages, such as the ability to link with computers and text messaging. They have a clarity of sound not often found with other wireless telephones. Unfortunately, hearing aid wearers may experience a buzzing sound due to the interference these telephones cause when they are in close proximity to some hearing aids and other hearing technology. Several consumer organizations, including Self Help for Hard of

Hearing People, are working with equipment providers and hearing aid manufacturers to address these problems. It is difficult to predict which aids and which telephones will be immune to interference; therefore, you must use trial and error when selecting a digital telephone.

Hearing the Telephone Ring

If you have difficulty hearing the telephone ring, an amplified telephone ringer can help. Some ringers are designed for easy listening by producing a lower tone. If you set the ringer at the greatest volume and this is not sufficient, you may want to install a device that flashes a light or causes a vibration when the phone rings (see chapter 19).

(21)

Cochlear Implants

IF YOU have a severe to profound hearing loss, are using appropriate hearing aids, and still have difficulty understanding speech, you may wish to explore the benefits of a cochlear implant. A cochlear implant is a device that is partially implanted into the cochlea to directly stimulate the auditory nerve. The device helps most recipients hear environmental sounds, improve their speechreading skills, monitor their own speech, and often understand voices without looking at the speaker. Some people even report that they can enjoy the sound of music again. It is not unusual for implant recipients to have full use of the telephone.

A cochlear implant is not a cure nor does it restore hearing to normal. It is an example of advanced technology that taps the retained potential of the hearing pathway, even in cases of profound deafness, by bypassing damaged hair cells to directly activate auditory nerve fibers. Many recipients say they function as well as people who have been effectively fitted with hearing aids.

How the Cochlear Implant Works

The cochlear implant works as follows: Sound waves enter the implant through the microphone located in an earpiece and are converted into electrical signals. The signals are sent to the wearable speech processor, which transforms each sound into a digital code. Because all sounds have their own distinctive "fingerprint" of energy peaks, they can be differentiated by the electrodes implanted in the cochlea. The digital signals are sent via radio waves to the electrodes, which in turn convert the information to electrical impulses that stimulate the nerve fibers of the auditory nerve; these impulses are transmitted to the brain where they are interpreted as sound.

The ideal candidate for a cochlear implant has a severe to profound sensorineural hearing loss in both ears, has tried hearing aids but still has difficulty with speech, and has no medical conditions that contraindicate the surgery. These medical contraindications are quite rare but include conditions that make a general anesthetic risky, such as severe coronary artery disease, a chronic pulmonary condition, or a genetic condition that interferes with the metabolism of anesthetic agents.

Success depends upon a number of factors such as patient motivation, the length of time the patient has had a hearing loss, and memory of sound and language. There have been dramatic improvements in cochlear implants in recent years; some adults who have the most advanced technology can understand 90 percent of words in sentences without speech-reading.

Cochlear implants have been in use for thirty years and have improved dramatically during the last five years. The Food and Drug Administration has approved three devices for use with adults and children.

If you are interested in exploring your candidacy for a cochlear implant, you will need several tests, some of which are the same as those you would have if you were assessing the potential benefits of a hearing aid. The first step is to have a hearing test and a hearing aid evaluation (see chapter 12). You also will need a medical and psychological evaluation to assess your medical suitability, level of motivation, and expectations. Other tests that help predict success of the procedure provide the implant team with needed information to determine which ear to implant via electrical stimulation of the auditory nerve.

The Actual Surgery

The surgery, performed under general anesthesia, is relatively pain free, takes two to three hours, and complications are rare. Most surgeries are performed as an outpatient procedure.

The surgeon makes an incision behind the ear, raises a skin flap to expose part of the mastoid bone, and drills a small depression in the bone to hold the receiver/stimulator (internal coil) in place. Then the surgeon threads an array of electrodes into the cochlea. The skin flap is sutured; healing takes about four weeks.

All cochlear implants have internal and external parts. The internal parts—internal coil and electrodes—are inserted during surgery. The external parts—microphone, speech processor, and external transmitter—are hooked together and linked via magnet to the internal parts after the incision has healed. At this time, the audiologist assesses the patient's ability to listen for sounds and adjusts controls in the speech processor. The speech processor is the size of a small calculator, and is worn externally as the speech decoder that drives the implant. The assessment may take several visits since the patient needs to adapt to new sounds that initially are different from the sounds heard through a hearing aid. With experience, many implant recipients note enhanced fidelity or sound quality.

Cost

Cochlear implants are expensive and currently cost from $40,000 to $50,000. This includes the evaluation, surgery, the device, hospital costs, fitting the device, and communication training. Many health insurance carriers, including Medicare, provide full or partial coverage for cochlear implant surgery and habilitation.

If you think you might be a candidate for a cochlear implant, talk to an otolaryngologist who may refer you to a specialist in this field. For a list of qualified specialists, contact:

The American Academy of Otolaryngology—
    Head and Neck Surgery, Inc.
One Prince Street
Alexandria, VA 22314-3357
(703) 836-4444
(703) 519-1585 TTY
www.entnet.org

In addition, lists of the centers that perform the surgery and follow-up services can be found on the web pages of the three cochlear implant manufacturers.

www.advancedbionics.com
www.cochlearcorporation.com
www.medel.com

(22)

Speechreading

MANY PEOPLE with hearing loss use their eyes to make up for what they cannot hear, especially if they have difficulty hearing speech as it normally sounds. You may have noticed that in addition to straining to hear what is being said, you also are using your eyes to get what your ears miss and that you seem to hear better when you see people's faces.

In the normal course of interacting with others, we all develop some degree of speechreading skill. Some of this skill involves lipreading—recognizing sounds by the shapes and movements of the speaker's mouth. Lipreading, however, is difficult because only 30 to 40 percent of speech is visible on the lips. Many sounds are made in the back of the throat, such as *k* and hard *g*. Also, many words have the same mouth movement and look the same on the lips, but sound different, such as *pat*, *bat*, and *mat*. Speechreading can be a little bit like taking a fill-in-the-blanks test, so paying attention to context as well as face and body movements is critical to good speechreading.

Your friends and family will often say, "You speechread, don't you?" Yes, you do, but you need to let them know that not all hard of hearing people read speech as easily and accurately as hearing people can listen to it, and not all hard of hearing people are skilled at speechreading. It is a skill that must be learned and practiced regularly. Some hard of hearing people are more successful than others because they hear better, and some simply have a special talent for speechreading.

When you speechread, it does not mean that you ignore your hearing; even a little bit of residual hearing can enhance speechreading ability. As it turns out, the sounds that are hardest to differentiate visually, like *p*, *b*, and *m*—because they are formed the same way on the lips—are the easiest ones to perceive through hearing. Conversely, the sounds that are likely to be the hardest to hear, like *s*, *f*, and *th* are the easiest ones to see. Good speechreaders combine all they can see and all they can hear for the purpose of improving speech comprehension.

People who have a regional accent, speak a language other than English, do not use much mouth movement, or have a mustache are more difficult to speechread. Unfamiliar topics and vocabulary as well as sudden changes of topic also can cause problems for the hard of hearing person. You will be able to improve your comprehension once you are familiar with the topic being discussed. You also may become better able to speechread individuals once you become accustomed to the way they speak.

Speechreading, like any new skill, is more likely to be acquired if you receive training, practice regularly, and have natural ability. Receiving encouragement from others helps, too. Unfortunately, classes are hard to find and are also usually short-term (eight to ten weeks), which is only a beginning. So you will have to work out a disciplined approach on your own. Try asking a relative or friend to work regularly with you, or seek out a local group that also is interested in speechreading, perhaps at a community center, senior center, of place of worship.

Speechreading videotapes and guidebooks are available, and some community colleges offer classes to help people refine their skills. Many of the chapters of Self Help for Hard of Hearing People offer speechreading courses.

(23)

Will an Oral Interpreter Help?

IF YOU depend on speechreading to get information, you probably have no trouble participating and following the flow of conversation in one-to-one and small group situations. However, when there is audience participation or when the speaker is on the stage or some distance away, you may find that speechreading can be difficult, if not impossible.

You may understand the speaker by sitting close and using assistive devices; audio loops or infrared systems also may help, when available. When neither of these is helpful, you might consider engaging an oral interpreter.

Well-meaning people may offer suggestions about using sign language interpreters to help you understand in large group situations, but learning sign language takes a great deal of patience and years of practice. An oral interpreter, however, might provide the support you need in certain situations.

What Is an Oral Interpreter?

Oral interpreters sit near you and repeat silently what is said at the time it is spoken, following two or three words behind the speaker. They simultaneously convey the mood and meaning of the message with expression and natural gestures. Oral interpreters are trained to mouth distinctly, may substitute a word that is easier to speechread, and may rephrase, all for the purpose of producing clear speech. If asked, the oral interpreters will use their voice to repeat the message if the speaker has unclear speech, a foreign accent, or wears a mustache or beard that might make speechreading difficult.

When to Consider Using an Oral Interpreter

If you are frustrated in meetings, seminars, and other situations in which you are not able to hear clearly, you may wish to consider using an oral interpreter. An oral interpreter is most helpful when the speaker is on the telephone or radio, providing narration that accompanies a TV or other audiovisual presentation, or has a foreign or regional accent. If you are unable to sit close to the speaker or if several people are speaking at the same time, using an oral interpreter can help your comprehension. Remember, however, that unless you are a skilled speechreader, you will not receive the entire message.

Many hard of hearing people who use residual hearing and speechreading to understand the speaker usually are not satisfied users of oral interpreters since the oral interpreter is several words behind the speaker.

How to Find an Oral Interpreter

If an interpreting service is not listed in your telephone book, you can contact the Registry of Interpreters for the Deaf (RID) for suggestions (see appendix A). Interpreters are professionals who graduate with a minimum of two years of training at a college or university and are certified or state approved based on written and performance evaluations. They are paid on an hourly basis. Fees vary from state to state.

It is your responsibility to pay for the interpreter if the service you need is personal, such as in a social situation. Under the Americans with Disabilities Act (see chapter 29), if you need an interpreter to participate in a program or service, the public accommodation, state or local government facility, or place of employment should pay the fee. For example, if you need an interpreter to understand hospital medical staff, the hospital should provide a qualified interpreter at no cost to you.

(24)

Assertive Communication

As a hard of hearing person, you may experience anger and frustration while trying to understand and be understood. You can cope with some of these communication frustrations you experience daily by learning simple assertiveness techniques.

Don't let the word assertive or the concept of assertive behavior scare you. There is a difference between *assertive* behavior and *aggressive* behavior. Assertiveness is a positive attribute. If you use assertive techniques, you will find that you can make things happen, change people's behavior, and, more importantly, change your own behavior. Aggressive behavior, on the other hand, is a negative approach and usually has negative results.

The following example will illustrate how you can communicate the same message in several ways, as well as the importance of communicating assertively.

You and your hearing companion arrive at a hotel and prepare to register. The desk clerk hands you a card and pen. You fill out the card and, as you wait for your room key, the desk clerk with head down asks for your credit card. You know the clerk is saying something, but you do not understand him and cannot see his face. How do you react?

1. You smile sweetly and act as if you didn't hear anything.
2. You ask your companion to tell you what the clerk said.
3. You angrily say something like, "Look at me when you speak to me, and speak louder!"

4. You calmly say, "I am hard of hearing. It will help me to hear you if you look at me when you speak."

Reactions 1 and 2 are examples of *passive behavior,* acting as if you understand what is going on when you don't. This behavior is often accompanied by a "sweet smile," a vague expression, letting someone else be your ears, and not letting other people know that you are hard of hearing. Passive behavior keeps you from dealing with the reality of your hearing loss. It makes you dependent on others. It often causes others to ignore you and to think of you as less capable than you are.

Reaction 3 is *aggressive behavior.* Examples of aggressive behavior are acting as if you are right and the world is wrong, demanding rather than asking for support, blaming others when you don't understand, dominating the conversation, and insisting on hearing everything. Hard of hearing people often use aggressive behavior to hide their disability. It does not solve communication problems; rather, it lowers self-esteem and may cause resentment in others, who may do what you ask but then may avoid interacting with you in the future.

Reaction 4 is an example of *assertive behavior.* Acting for yourself, accepting your hearing loss, taking responsibility for your actions, and communicating clearly to let others know what they can do to be helpful are elements of assertive behavior.

Assertive behavior allows you to act in your own best interests, to stand up for yourself, to express your feelings comfortably, and to exercise your rights while not infringing on the rights of others. With assertive behavior, you say: "I know I have a problem. I am asking for your help, and I am telling you what I need."

Assertive behavior is not easy. It takes much practice, but after a while, what you say and what you do becomes second nature.

Body Language

Assertiveness is not only verbal, meaning what you say and how you say it. Many other nonverbal factors—known as body language—come into play, including,

- eye contact
- body posture
- distance/physical contact
- gestures
- facial expressions
- voice tone, inflection, and volume
- pace of speech
- timing

Body language can send a very different message than the words you are saying. When your body says one thing and your voice says another, the body language prevails.

Taking Responsibility

Remember your hearing problem is just that—*your* problem. It is not anyone else's problem. It is your responsibility to take charge of the situation and help yourself and, at the same time, not make others feel uncomfortable. When you have recognized and accepted that you have a hearing loss, have had your hearing tested and evaluated, and have purchased hearing aids, you have already taken a large measure of responsibility (see chapter 25).

Being assertive can make a big difference in your life. You can become more assertive by saying what is on your mind, expressing yourself honestly, and respecting your rights and the rights of others. Getting what you want and what you need is not always easy. Getting what you need and not infringing on the rights of others is an art.

If you want to learn more about assertive techniques that will help you deal with your hearing loss and with other general situations, you will find books and videos on this subject in your library. Courses on assertiveness are often taught at community colleges and offered by many Self Help for Hard of Hearing People chapters.

(25)

Tips for Improving Communication

ONCE FRIENDS, relatives, and others with whom you interact are aware that you have a hearing loss, they will want to know how best to communicate with you. Being specific about your needs will provide an opportunity for you to help others while helping yourself. Don't just say "I have a hearing loss." Tell people exactly what they can do to help.

You are the primary decision maker when choosing the appropriate environment for communication. You need to tell people with whom you are talking that you can't hear well when the water is running, the television is on, their back is turned, when others in the room are carrying on an animated conversation, and in any situation that causes a problem for you. A quiet place with no background noise is priority number one. Lighting is important, too; it should be on the speaker's face in order for you to receive maximum benefit. Since sound disperses with distance, you should get as close as you can to the speaker. If appropriate, encourage the speaker to use facial expressions and gestures.

Note: One way to ensure that good communication continues is to provide feedback. Let others know what they are doing right. Also, let them know what could be done differently in order to enhance communication. Saying "Thank you" is the best way to provide positive feedback.

Below are a few tips for improving communication that you can use to educate other people and take control of your life. Ask them to do the following:

- Please get my attention before speaking to me.
  Ask the speaker to tap you on the shoulder, wave, or use another gesture before beginning to speak.
- Please give me a clue.
  Knowing what the topic of conversation is can help you understand better. Ask the speaker to say something such as "Lunch. Where shall we have lunch?"
- Please face me.
  Asking the speaker to look at you when talking helps you to hear and speechread more effectively. Position yourself so that the speaker's face is not in the shadows.
- Please speak slowly and clearly.
  Explain that the speaker need not shout nor exaggerate speech. Exaggeration and overemphasis of words distort lip movements, making speechreading more difficult.

- Please rephrase rather than repeat.
  If you do not understand the first time, ask the speaker to rephrase the sentence. You may only miss one or two words, and repetition may help you understand the message the second time around. However, rephrasing often is a better solution.
- Please talk directly to me.
  If you find that people often talk to your hearing companion or spouse when they should be talking to you, be assertive and ask that they talk directly to you. You may need to coach them, but your efforts will pay off with positive results and the communication you need.
- Please don't cover your mouth when talking to me.
  People often talk when eating, chewing on a pencil, or in some way obscuring their mouth. Let them know that this makes speechreading difficult.
- Please turn off the television or radio.
  Background noise is one main reason for not hearing well. Help yourself by requesting that noise be turned down or off before engaging in conversation. You might also suggest moving to a quieter spot.
- Please don't shout.
  Shouting makes things worse. It distorts the face and mouth of the speaker often making speechreading impossible. If you wear a hearing aid, shouting causes increased vibrations and distorts sound.

In addition to helping other people learn what they can do to facilitate communication, you can do the following:

- Pay attention.
  You need to watch, listen, and concentrate to follow conversation. Daydreaming cuts off communication.

- Concentrate on the speaker.
  If the conversation is important, pay close attention to the speaker. You become a better conversationalist because you focus on one person at a time and are not disturbed by other people and events.
- Look for visual cues.
  Watch for facial expressions, gestures, and body language, which are signs that indicate if the conversation is proceeding well.
- Ask for written cues if needed.
  Always carry a notepad and pencil. If you are really stuck, ask the speaker to write key word(s) for you. Sometimes a key word will put the conversation back on track.
- Don't interrupt. Let conversation flow awhile to gain more meaning.
  Sometimes you pick up the missed key word a few sentences later so that what is being discussed makes sense. Give the exchange a chance before you interrupt, but if you are lost, explain and ask for repetition or rephrasing.

(26)

Rearranging Your Home Environment

IN YOUR own home you can make several changes that make hearing and understanding speech easier. Arrange the furniture where you most frequently sit and converse so that you are close to the person or persons with whom you talk.

Position your chair so that your back is to the light source and the light from a window or lamp is on the other person's face. Consider installing better lighting if yours is recessed, since this type of lighting creates shadows and makes speechreading difficult.

You may wish to arrange your chair so that you are able to see people entering a room. This will prevent you from being startled if you can't hear someone come in and frightened if you are tapped on the shoulder from behind.

Background and other noises are often disturbing, so when conversing, turn the television, radio, or stereo down or off. If you are in someone else's home or office, don't be afraid to explain that you will hear better if there is no background noise. Noise reverberation also makes hearing and understanding difficult. Consider dampening reverberation with sound-absorbing material such as carpeting, draperies, and upholstered furniture.

If you can hear better in one ear than the other, position the speaker close to the better ear. Remember to do this when you are in a restaurant or at the theater, also.

If you have difficulty understanding the voices on television, consider purchasing a TV listening device that will enable you to hear without turning the volume too loud for other listeners (see chapter 18).

If you have trouble understanding on the telephone, investigate the many telephone devices on the market that meet the varying needs of hard of hearing people. Choosing the right device depends on your needs and the environment in which you will use it (see chapter 20).

If you have trouble hearing the telephone ring or someone knocking on your door, consider installing visual signaling devices to compensate for your hearing loss that at the same time allow you to gain a greater sense of awareness. Visual signaling devices—some very inexpensive, others more elaborate—will provide visual alerts such as flashing lights, or vibrations, to indicate the source of a sound such as timers on ovens, a washing machine cycle ending, and other household sounds that help you in your daily work around the house. A visual smoke detector is another device that will provide a sense of confidence and security at home (see chapter 19).

You may even consider remodeling. If so, contemplate an open-space design, which is better than closed rooms because it allows you to visually keep track of what is going on in all parts of your living area.

If you need glasses, wear them. You use your eyes more than ever when you lose your hearing. Your sense of sight becomes more critical in order to compensate for what you don't hear. If low vision is reducing your ability to cope with hearing loss and communicate effectively, you need to make adjustments in many areas. A dual sensory loss requires learning how to use whatever hearing and vision remain, together with some additional strategies (see chapter 25).

(27)

Living Alone

PEOPLE WITH hearing loss must face a number of challenges and responsibilities in order to live alone and function independently: using the telephone; hearing the doorbell and wake-up alarm; enjoying television, radio, and stereo;

and dealing with health care, repairs, and other service providers. How can you remain in control of your life and your decisions?

1. You can enjoy an independent and relaxed lifestyle by acknowledging your hearing loss.
2. If you use a hearing aid, wear it every day—not only for special occasions.
3. Learn about the many assistive devices that can be used in concert with hearing aids.
4. Consider refining your speechreading skills.
5. Learn techniques for modifying and controlling your living and social environments.
6. Let other people know that you have a hearing loss and explain your communication needs clearly.

By discovering new ways to adapt you can participate fully in the world around you.

If you are one of the 25 percent of people with a hearing loss who live alone, the following strategies might help you learn how to remain independent.

• Hearing the telephone and the doorbell
A variety of alerting devices and systems that use a flashing light or vibrations are available to alert you to door knocks, doorbells, telephones, burglar alarms, smoke and fire alarms, and other sounds you may have difficulty hearing.
• Hearing on the telephone
Telephone listening devices can increase the loudness of sound coming through the telephone. They can be used with or without a hearing aid. If you have difficulty hearing on the telephone, a telephone with built-in vol-

ume control or an amplified handset might be the solution. You may want to try a portable amplifier when you are away from your home phone. If your hearing loss is more profound, consider using a TTY as well as telecommunications relay services. Look into e-mail, voice mail, and caller ID, services that allow you to get information visually (see chapter 20).

- Waking up at a specified time
  Specialized wake-up alarms for hard of hearing people include clocks, bed vibrators, and timers. Clocks that use a flashing light for the alarm are useful for people easily awakened by light. For heavy sleepers, several kinds of bed-vibrating units may be helpful. Some can be placed under a pillow or mattress. Some are small enough for travel. Timers or clocks with built-in electrical outlets allow you to choose whether to use a light or vibrator.

- Listening to television, radio, and stereo
  TV, radio, and stereo listening devices allow you to increase the loudness of sound without disturbing other people or damaging your residual hearing. Some devices can be connected to the TV, radio, or stereo when using an audio input hearing aid, by using earphones instead of a hearing aid, or by using an induction loop. A TV caption decoder allows the viewer to see text of TV dialogue of programs that are captioned. All TV sets that are thirteen inches and larger, manufactured after July 1, 1993, have a built-in chip that allows users to see captions without a decoder (see chapter 18).

- Receiving emergency warnings
  Many hard of hearing people worry about not hearing the alarm from their smoke detectors. Some smoke detectors combine a built-in horn and a strobe light; others

have a separate horn that plugs into an electrical outlet in the bedroom or elsewhere in the house. A lamp, strobe, or vibrating device also can plug into a portable receiver. Emergency alarm devices can automatically call the fire department and give the person's address when a smoke detector goes off. Other emergency alarm devices call an emergency service (police, fire, or ambulance) and play a recorded message at the press of a button (see chapter 20).

Problems Away from Home

- In the hospital
  Hospitalization, while often stressful for many, can be even more disturbing for a hard of hearing person whose anxieties are compounded by the fear of not hearing or understanding questions and instructions, announcements, and directions. While all patients in hospitals need advocates, your needs as a hard of hearing patient are even more critical (see chapter 33).
- While traveling
  If you need and want to travel alone for business or personal enjoyment, you can continue to remain independent and effective by careful planning and exercising special techniques (see chapter 34).
- At the hairdresser/barber
  Difficulty communicating while having your hair washed, cut, and styled can be overcome with a little effort. By alerting the hairdresser/barber that discussions must be held and decisions made before you remove your hearing aid(s), you will be using specialized communication techniques and educating others at the same time.

Hearing Dogs

You may wish to consider a hearing dog that is trained to respond to sounds and alert you to them (see chapter 19).

A Final Word of Advice

Try various devices and systems and evaluate them to find what works best for your level of hearing loss with and without a hearing aid. Also, learn special communication techniques that allow you to remain independent. Remember that many hard of hearing people are living alone successfully, and so can you.

(28)

The International Symbol of Access for Hearing Loss

You HAVE a new friend: the International Symbol of Access for Hearing Loss (see figure 8). Used worldwide, this symbol identifies locations where communication access is provided.

The symbol is typically white with a blue background. You will see it on public phones and know that they are hearing-aid compatible and have amplification. You will see it posted in meeting rooms and in places of entertainment and worship to indicate that the room is equipped with an assistive listening system. You will see it posted on patients'

Figure 8. The International Symbol of Access for Hearing Loss

doors in hospitals to alert hospital personnel to the fact that the patient has a hearing loss.

Wherever you see it, you will know that people are aware of hearing loss and have responded by providing communication accessibility.

(29)

What Are Your Legal Rights?

IN THE past, many older Americans experienced age discrimination in the workplace. They were passed over during hiring and often for promotion. When they also had a hearing loss, they may have experienced double discrimination. Because of recent legislation, this discrimination is occurring less frequently. Still, many people with disabilities, including those with hearing loss, are unaware of the several laws that protect their civil rights. Others are reluctant to ask for accommodations that would help them participate in everyday activities. The Americans with Disabilities Act

(ADA) (Public Law 101-336) is comprehensive federal legislation affirming the rights of persons with disabilities to equal access.

The Americans with Disabilities Act

The ADA, enacted in 1990 to protect people with physical or mental disabilities, ensures that all Americans have access to employment (Title I), public services and public transportation (Title II), public accommodations (Title III), and telecommunications (Title IV). The ADA states that no individual may be discriminated against on the basis of disability in the "full and equal enjoyment" of the services or facilities of any place of "public accommodation." Because hearing loss is considered a disability, you are protected under the law.

If you are employed or seeking employment, the ADA guarantees you equal opportunity. Employers must reasonably accommodate the disabilities of qualified applicants or current employees, unless an undue hardship would result.

You should have access to all local, state, and federal government facilities, services, and communication. Public buses and bus stations, and trains and train stations, need to comply with the ADA. Airlines are covered by the Air Carriers Access Act, but airports must provide accessibility under the ADA.

You should have access to public accommodations. This means that hotels, restaurants, theaters, retail stores, museums, libraries, and parks must include services that make it easier for you to hear. Hospitals, pharmacies, and doctors' offices also must comply. Places of worship and private clubs are exempt from the ADA; many of these, however, provide access for people with hearing loss.

Telephone companies must provide free relay service to people with hearing loss who use TTYs or similar devices twenty-four hours a day, seven days a week.

If You Believe That You Have Been Discriminated Against

If you believe that you have been discriminated against, you have several options. Assuming you have exhausted all methods of negotiation with your employer, facility manager, etc., it is a good idea to first try mediation. This can be done through local mediation centers, conflict resolution services, and legal offices specializing in disputes. This strategy has proved successful in avoiding litigation. If mediation fails, you have the following legal recourse:

- In Employment: You may file a complaint with the Equal Employment Opportunity Commission (EEOC).
- In Public Accommodations: You can bring a private lawsuit to obtain court orders to stop discrimination, but money damages cannot be awarded. Or you can file a complaint with the U.S. Attorney General, who may file lawsuits to stop discrimination and obtain money damages and penalties.
- In Transportation: You may file a complaint with the U.S. Department of Transportation or bring a private lawsuit.
- In State and Local Government Operations: You may file a complaint with federal agencies to be designated by the U.S. Attorney General or bring a private lawsuit.
- In Telecommunications: You may file a complaint with the Federal Communications Commission (FCC).

Other Relevant Legislation

The Hearing Aid Compatibility Act of 1988 stipulates that all telephones manufactured in the United States or imported for use in the United States must provide internal means for effective use with hearing aids that are designed to be compatible with telephones that meet established technical standards for hearing aid compatibility.

The Television Decoder Circuitry Act of 1990 stipulates that all televisions with screens thirteen inches and larger manufactured since 1993 must contain a built-in decoder chip.

The Rehabilitation Act of 1973 states that all people have a right to equal opportunities. Title V of the act specifies that facilities and programs receiving federal funds be accessible to all disabled persons. Under Section 502 of Title V, buildings and facilities that are designed, constructed, altered, or leased with federal funds must be communication accessible. Section 504 of the act deals with federally funded programs and activities. The act prohibits discrimination against people with disabilities such as employees, participants, or viewers.

Below are several web sites related to the legal rights of people with hearing loss.

The Federal Communications Commission (FCC) in Washington, D.C., regulates telecommunications, which are of vital importance to people with hearing loss. You can get further information on telephones, access to the Internet and other communications issues affecting people with hearing loss at www.fcc.gov.

The U.S. Access Board is responsible for implementing the physical barriers aspect of the Americans with Disabilities Act. You can get information on suggested technologies for making movies accessible to people with hearing loss at www.access-board.gov.

Self Help for Hard of Hearing People (SHHH) is an organization devoted to the needs of people with hearing loss, their families and friends. SHHH is involved in education and advocacy for the rights of people with hearing loss. Check out the public policy page at www.shhh.org.

(30)

Hearing in Restaurants

MANY SOCIAL and business activities take place at mealtimes and in restaurants. It is difficult for most people to watch their food and the face of their companion(s) simultaneously, but for people with hearing loss, it can cause greater problems and significant frustration.

If your dining companion is a close relative or friend whose voice you are used to, and the subject matter you will be discussing is familiar, you may have no problem hearing. If, however, the meal is for business purposes, with someone you have met recently, with a larger group, or with someone who also has a hearing loss, you will communicate more successfully by taking a number of factors into account when choosing a restaurant. These include noise level, lighting, and seating.

Most people choose restaurants for the quality and variety of food and for the service, ambience, and price. Hard of hearing people need to take other things into consideration when dining out in order to increase their ability to understand conversation.

Below are a few suggestions for making your restaurant dining experience more enjoyable.

- Call ahead, if possible. Tell the person accepting the reservation that you are hard of hearing and would like a table in a quiet spot. You may need to explain that "quiet" means little or no noise from behind, not near the air conditioning/heating unit or loudspeaker, and certainly not in the center of the room. A corner table or a booth in the back is often a good choice.
- Timing is important. The best times for lower noise levels are before and after peak hours. Not only are restaurants crowded at noon and 6:30 p.m., but service is usually rushed.
- Choose a restaurant with good lighting. Some restaurants have low levels of lighting, which can make it difficult to speechread and see facial expressions. Music often accompanies soft lights. Don't hesitate to ask the waiter to turn down or turn off the music if a speaker near you is causing difficulty hearing.
- Choose the seat at the table that will maximize your ability to hear the conversation. If you hear better in one ear than in the other, ask your companion or the person you most wish to hear to sit on the better side. A seat against a wall is a good choice because you will not have sound coming to you from behind. If the restaurant has windows or bright lighting, be sure that your back is to the light so that your companions' faces are not in the shadows.
- Restaurants often offer specials. Ask the waiter if these are written down so that you can read them; if not, ask the waiter to stand closer to you so that you can speechread and hear better.

- If you own an FM system or another one-on-one communicator, be sure to take it with you to facilitate conversation with your dinner companions and the waiter.
- If you are unable to make a reservation beforehand and find yourself in a noisy restaurant or at a noisy table where communication would be difficult, and it is important that you be able to understand what is being said, consider leaving and finding another restaurant.

While most restaurant personnel are helpful and understanding, you need to tell them that you have a hearing loss and what they can do to help you hear. When they provide help, show your gratitude; when they don't, you can make your dissatisfaction known, courteously, but firmly.

Drive-Thrus

For those of you who enjoy fast-food dining, the drive-thru procedure can be challenging since you are unable to see the face of the person taking your order, and the audio system often is poor quality. In order to take advantage of this convenient way to get a meal without leaving your automobile, be prepared to place your order when you hear the "squawk" at the drive-up box. Speak clearly and provide information as completely as possible, ending with the statement "That's all, thank you." Drive on to the payment window, where the order taker will relay any unanswered questions. You may have a delay at the window, but the procedure may be faster than standing in line inside and useful when you are tired or in a hurry.

Bon Appetit!

Eating Out at a Restaurant
Tips for Hard of Hearing Guests

- Call and make a reservation ahead of time. Ask for a table or booth in a well-lit, quiet area.
- Make your reservation for "off" hours. Avoid peak times like Friday or Saturday night, or noon to one o'clock during the week.
- Avoid a restaurant with live entertainment.
- Keep your group small.
- At fast-food establishments, decide ahead what you are going to order.
- Tell the hostess and waiter/waitress that you are hard of hearing.
- Avoid areas close to the kitchen, air-conditioners, and other noisy equipment.
- When seated, position yourself near the person you wish to communicate with; if possible, sit with your back to a wall and don't face a window or bright light. Avoid tables in the center of room.
- If an amplifier to a PA system is near you, ask if it can be turned down.
- If "specials" are available, ask to see a list that you can read.
- Use your own personal assistive listening devices, such as one-on-one communicators.
- Discourage more than one conversation at a time among the group.
- Keep your sense of humor.
- Give thanks to those who assist you.

Reprinted with permission from the SHHH Rochester Restaurant Committee.

(31)

Hearing in Theaters and Movies

IF YOU enjoyed theater productions and movies before you lost your hearing, you will wish to continue to enjoy them now. Since the passage of the Americans with Disabilities Act (ADA), most theaters and movie houses (and public facilities in general, including sports arenas) have installed systems designed to accommodate people with hearing losses. One way to ensure that accessibility to movies and theaters continues is to use these systems and let theater owners and managers know if they are working well.

Some theaters advertise in local newspaper movie guides that they have special audio systems in place. Others fail to advertise so you may need to call and inquire if the theater has a system available. The newspaper may also tell what kinds of devices are available. Most theaters have headphones. Some have neck loops for hard of hearing people who have T-switches on their hearing aids. Some have the Rear Window System.

If you have not been able to inquire about assistive devices beforehand, look for signs indicating that assistive devices are available when you arrive at the theater. The International Symbol of Access for Hearing Loss often lets consumers know that the theater is accessible to people with hearing loss (see chapter 28). If no signs are posted, ask about accessibility at the ticket counter.

Even though theaters may be in compliance with the ADA, you and other consumers with hearing loss who have high expectations for the equipment may come away dissatisfied. Theater personnel sometimes are uninformed or poorly trained because the information they receive about assistive devices may be incorrect or insufficient. Imagine what that is like for a first-time user. As a consumer, it will benefit you to become informed so that you can help educate the theater personnel and thus receive maximum benefit from the equipment.

Headphones

The most often used pieces of equipment in movie theaters are wireless, light, and easy to use headphones designed to receive infrared waves. The earphones are attached to a panel displaying a switch and volume control. A thumbwheel can adjust the volume, which operates only when an infrared emitter, usually mounted above the screen, is in operation. A diode at the base of each earphone receives the wireless radiation of the infrared emitter through a hidden eye that faces the screen as you are seated in the theater. The only precaution is that the eye not be obscured by clothes, hands, a person, or object because this may cut off the reception of sound from the infrared emitter.

Rear Window System

The Rear Window System has made the provision of hidden captions in movie theaters possible. The system provides closed captions for people who need them without displaying the captions to the entire audience. The captions are not on the film itself; they are on a floppy disk or CD that plays in synchronization with the film and can be made visible only to those patrons who choose to see them. The system displays reversed captions on a light-emitting diode text display, which is mounted in the rear of the theater. Patrons use transparent acrylic panels that can be attached to their seats and reflect the captions so that they appear superimposed on or beneath the movie screen. The panels are portable, enabling the user to sit anywhere in the theater.

In order to borrow a device and ensure that it will be returned, you may have to leave a driver's license or other identification with the employee at the ticket counter. It is illegal for theaters to charge for use of the receivers. When you return the equipment at the end of the performance, be sure to let personnel know how much you appreciate having it available. If it worked well for you, mention that. If it is inadequate or not in working order, let the manager of the theater know that the equipment is not providing adequate support or needs repair. When the theater advertises that it provides accommodation for hard of hearing people, it should do so; therefore, it is not unreasonable to ask for a refund if the system is not working properly and you have to leave. If systems are not used, or if they are not doing the job, then nothing will be done to improve them unless you and others speak up.

Above all, don't let the stigma factor of hearing loss keep you from enjoying movies and theater productions. It may be more comfortable to rent a captioned video and stay at home—and this too is an option—but socializing and sharing with others is an important part of remaining active.

(32)

Hearing in Places of Worship

IF YOU have difficulty hearing in your place of worship and are unable to participate fully in the service or meetings, consider talking to your minister, priest, or rabbi about your feelings of being "left out" and the impact this has on your spiritual life. Explain that the inability to hear religious services, announcements, and at special ceremonies relating to celebrations of life results in a deep sense of deprivation and loss. Emphasize that an improved listening environment could provide accessibility for you and other hard of hearing members of the congregation. This is an opportunity for you to be an advocate for yourself and at the same time fulfill a requirement of your faith to act on behalf of others.

If your place of worship does not have an assistive listening system (see chapter 18), let your clergy know that even though places of worship are exempt from the Americans with Disabilities Act, more and more congregations are employing the use of these systems to help people who are hard of hearing. Some places of worship have systems that are not being used. There could be several reasons for this: The system is not being advertised so congregants are unaware that it is in place, hard of hearing people do not like to be conspicuous by wearing a device, or, often, the system is inadequate or not functioning properly. For example, FM and infrared systems require continual attention to ensure that receivers are in working order, and audio loop systems may not be powerful enough to meet the needs of worshipers.

The mere presence of an audio system is not enough to include hard of hearing people in the activities of the congregation. Members of the congregation need to be educated about the availability of the system and how to use it. Ushers must be trained to guide worshipers to reserved pews that have been installed with devices and offer instruction for their use. They also need to know what seating provides optimal listening if loop systems are installed. You, as an advocate, should use the systems and encourage others to do the same.

Often a system has been installed in the nave of the structure. It is equally important that a system be placed in other locations. Explain that when lecture halls and meeting rooms are not equipped with special devices that make dialogue accessible, you miss out on the comfort and inspiration of a spiritual community.

If your place of worship wants to investigate installing a system, a good place to begin is to identify precise requirements. The administration should survey the congregation to determine the number of personal receivers, earphones, earbuds, and neck loops needed. It is important also to survey members who have stopped attending services because they did not hear well. However, a survey should not be used to determine whether a system should be installed.

The system considered for installation by your place of worship should accommodate members of the congregation who do not wear hearing aids as well as those who do.

The church administration may need guidelines for making the house of worship accessible. Refer them to *One Voice*, a handbook provided by the Rochester chapter of Self Help for Hard of Hearing People.* The administration also may

---

*For information about the *One Voice* project and to obtain a handbook call (585) 266-7890 or visit SHHH Rochester on the web at www.mail@shhh-rochester-ny.org.

not know where to buy a system. SHHH, hearing clinics, audiologists, and sound system installers can help identify suppliers. You and other hard of hearing congregants should insist on being present during the system demonstrations before purchase and also during the trial period after a system is installed to ensure satisfactory operation; otherwise, installers may not be aware of your needs.

(33)

Hearing in the Hospital

HOSPITALIZATION, while often stressful for many, can be even more disturbing to a hard of hearing person whose anxieties are compounded by the fear of not hearing or understanding questions, instructions, and announcements. These concerns are not unfounded. If you have difficulty communicating with hospital staff members, it may cause misunderstandings that can affect your treatment and lead to undesirable consequences. Therefore, as a hard of hearing patient, it is essential that you make every effort to establish good communication with the nurses, doctors, and other members of the health care staff.

Preadmission

Use your preadmission visit to inform the admissions office and other hospital personnel of your hearing loss and discuss your communication needs. The preadmission form may ask if you have a hearing loss; if it does not, you should note your hearing loss on the form anyway. Request materials such as brochures and pamphlets that describe the services and equipment available for people with hearing loss. Some hospitals, for example, provide captioned television, one-on-one communicators, and amplified telephones.

In the Hospital

Once you are settled into your room, begin your effort to establish good communication by making sure that your chart is labeled to alert health care providers that you are hard of hearing. With your consent, a card or the International Symbol of Access for Hearing Loss should be placed on the door (see chapter 28). As the nurses and other members of the hospital staff come to your room to greet you, take the opportunity to discuss with each of them your preferred method of communication. If you use assistive devices other than your hearing aid, such as a one-on-one communicator, captioned TV, amplified telephone, or personal FM system, explain to them how the devices operate.

It is not enough to tell people "I am hard of hearing." Educate them. Tell them how to communicate with you by giving them specific strategies such as "try to get my attention before speaking." You may need to repeat this information because staff members may forget, and you may be communicating with different personnel on different shifts. Be patient and polite, but be persistent.

If you do not understand messages over the intercom, ask that information specific for you be delivered face to face. You might suggest that a note or the access symbol be posted at the nurses' station as a reminder when communicating important general information.

It also is important that you understand what the hospital personnel are telling you about your medical condition.

If you don't understand what is being communicated, ask to have the information repeated or provided in writing. If you bluff, you may miss important information. Ask about the medications that are prescribed for you because some medications are ototoxic and may adversely affect your hearing (see chapter 8). You may wish to have instructions about medications repeated in order to ensure that you clearly understand dosages, purposes, and procedures—and don't hesitate to ask for written instructions.

In addition, if you wear hearing aids, you or a family member or friend should instruct the hospital personnel about the insertion, care, and use of aids as well as the care and testing of batteries, if you are unable to do this for yourself. Tell the staff that when you remove your hearing aids at night or in the shower, you will not be able to hear. Also, be sure that when you remove your hearing aids, they are placed where they won't be lost or damaged and where you can find them easily.

Before and After Surgery

Surgery presents another challenge for a hard of hearing patient since it is difficult, if not impossible, to understand what is being said when the surgical staff members are wearing masks. Inform your surgeon, and particularly your anesthesiologist, of your hearing loss. You may wish to wear your hearing aid during surgery. This is allowed, depending on the type of surgery and equipment used during the procedure. Discuss this with the anesthesiologist. If it is not possible to wear your hearing aid in the operating room, wear it up to the last minute and have a zip-lock bag handy for the aid that is well labeled with your name and room number. You may request that surgical personnel communicate information and instructions before covering their lips.

In the recovery room following surgery, you may encounter personnel who are not aware of your hearing loss. As the anesthesia wears off, you will want to have someone with you who knows how best to communicate with you. Arrange this ahead of time.

As an Outpatient

When you have medical procedures performed in diagnostic laboratories or X-ray departments as an outpatient, you can make the experience less stressful by taking the following steps:

- Tell the receptionist your name and explain that you are hard of hearing.
- Because you may not hear your name when called, ask that someone approach you to get your attention.
- Ask to have "Hard of Hearing" shown prominently on all your medical records as a reminder to the various staff members who interact with you.
- Express your appreciation for the attention you have received.

In the Emergency Room

There are times when you may be unable to prepare for a hospital stay, such as in the event of an accident or sudden illness. It is important for you to plan for hospital emergencies because hearing loss can pose special challenges and risks for you and for the person providing emergency care. Quick recognition that you are hard of hearing is important so that staff members can provide adequate and appropriate care. Keep a card in your wallet that indicates you have a hearing loss and whether you communicate through speechreading or use an assistive device. Remind family members who may accompany you for emergency admission to alert the staff about your hearing loss and how the staff can best communicate with you.

During an emergency, if you are unable to hear because your hearing aid has been damaged or is not working, you may wish to ask for a voice amplifier (a one-on-one communicator). Emergency room personnel may not know that people who are hard of hearing need amplification to communicate rather than a sign language interpreter. However, some hard of hearing patients may need the services of an oral interpreter (see chapter 23). Some hospital emergency rooms have prepared cards with written questions to have ready for these situations.

Other Difficult Situations

In addition to not hearing your name called while waiting for tests or examinations, misunderstanding important details of your diagnosis and prognosis, incorrectly interpreting specific questions concerning health care and medications, and missing what is being said when medical personnel are wearing surgical masks, you may find the following medical situations difficult and should be prepared to address them:

- When you are having a procedure related to your eyes, you may need special consideration because people with hearing loss need to see in order to understand what is being said.
- When your back is to the speaker, such as when you are in bed, receiving an injection, or being pushed in a wheelchair or on a gurney, you will need to remind personnel that you need to see them in order to understand them.

- When having a chest X-ray, ask the radiology technician to flash a light to let you know when to hold your breath.

Items to Ask for During a Hospital Stay

Hospitals are required by the Americans with Disabilities Act and Section 504 of the Rehabilitation Act to have assistive listening devices, such as one-on-one communicators, on the premises for their use. You may wish to ask for a telephone with a visible alert, an amplified telephone, or a TTY; a caption decoder for TV or a TV with a captioning chip; and an International Symbol of Access for Hearing Loss for the door of your room.

Items to Take to the Hospital with You

The following items can be helpful in making your hospital stay less stressful:

- A small night light to facilitate speechreading at night
- A supply of SHHH Communication Tips pocket cards to distribute to hospital personnel (available from SHHH; see chapter 41 for contact information)
- Your personal communication equipment
- Extra hearing aid batteries
- A storage container labeled with your name for your hearing aids
- A pen and paper to use when you are not able to wear your hearing aids

(34)

Hearing When Traveling

TRAVEL IS an enjoyable option, particularly during retirement years. As a hard of hearing person, traveling alone or with others does not need to be stressful. The secret to successful travel is anticipation and assertiveness. Think about what you need in order to feel safe and to remain independent when away from home. Before you leave home, plan strategies for getting what you need.

Away from home, you will have many occasions to interact for the first time with strangers, including hotel staff, shopkeepers, and other travelers. If you let them know at the outset that you do not hear well and what they can do to make communication easier, you will find that most people are happy to work with you to facilitate understanding.

Hotels and Motels

When Making Your Reservation

In addition to inquiring about such things as king-size beds and the cost of an extra cot, request specific accommodations such as amplified telephones and TTYs, alerting devices, and closed-captioned TV. A number of equipment distributors work with hoteliers and hospitality franchises nationwide to make their establishments hearing accessible. Some of the equipment is permanently installed in rooms; other items are quickly installed after check-in. If the facility does not have these items, remind the manager that the Americans with Disabilities Act requires hotels and motels with five or more sleeping rooms to provide reasonable accommodations, including those mentioned above.

On Arrival

If you have not requested these beforehand, request amplified telephones, alerting devices, and closed-captioned TV. If the establishment has this equipment, ask to have it installed in your room. It doesn't hurt to commend the establishment for providing these items.

Check-in also provides an opportunity to educate staff about ways to communicate with hard of hearing people. Because the registration area is usually noisy, ask personnel to face you and speak clearly (see chapter 25).

Using the Telephone

The telephone is essential for most travelers. Hotels are required to carry accessible telephones, but this could be a telephone in the lobby. Inquire about telephones when you make your reservations. If the establishment does not have accessible telephones in the room, consider going elsewhere. If, however, you must stay at a particular establishment and the hotel cannot provide a hearing aid-compatible telephone or an amplified handset, you may wish to carry a portable telephone amplifier with you. Some travelers like to carry a portable TTY (see chapter 20).

Watching Television

In the United States, hotels with five or more sleeping rooms are supposed to have captioned television in 4 percent of the rooms. If you need a decoder, request that one be hooked up in your room, or request a room with a new television with the decoding chip.

On Tour (Guided and On Your Own)

Traveling in groups does not have to be a frustrating experience for the hard of hearing person. When on a guided tour, position yourself as close as possible to the guide in order to maximize what you hear and also to see the guide's lip movements. If you own a portable FM system, bring it with you and ask the guide to use the transmitter. Explain how it works and show the guide how to wear the microphone. Some Scandinavian countries frequently have induction loops on tour buses. In art galleries and museums and at historic places, ask if you may borrow the guidebook used by guides, if available, or if you might use the written script for the audiotapes for self-guided tours.

Making Travel More Accessible in the Future

Accessibility in public places improves daily because people with disabilities, including hard of hearing people, are requesting access. If you need support services, ask for them. You also should praise people in places that do provide services. When you see a need for improvement, offer constructive criticism and recommendations. You can make a difference by offering suggestions such as: "If the video were captioned, it could be better understood by people with hearing loss and those who speak a language other than English." Because many national parks are working to upgrade facilities for people with hearing loss, inquire about the status, and use the equipment so that they will continue to work to accommodate hard of hearing people.

Traveling in a Car

Whether you are the driver or the passenger, you likely will want to converse with companions on long trips while keeping

Note: People with disabilities, including those with hearing loss, are eligible for the Golden Access Passport from the National Parks Service, which provides free entrance to recreational areas and parks in the United States.

your eyes on the road. A one-on-one communicator will enable you to carry on a conversation easily (see chapter 18). If you have an audio jack on your car radio, a neck loop enables you to listen to the radio or taped book.

Safety is always important. If you are not able to hear sirens or your signal light when driving, you could be placing yourself in a dangerous situation unnecessarily. Two signaling devices can help you. An emergency response indicator is a signaling device for the automobile that turns on a light when emergency vehicles such as fire, police, or ambulance sirens or car horns are nearby. A turn signal reminder can alert you that your left-right signal is "on." Several automobile manufacturers offer a rebate for the complete cost of these devices to hard of hearing and deaf people who have purchased a car manufactured after 1994.

Traveling on an Airplane

It is not easy for a hard of hearing person to hear in noisy places, and airports and airplanes can be especially noisy. When all goes well, the signs in the airport provide sufficient information about flight times, gate numbers, cancellations, and locations. However, the unexpected, such as a gate change or a delay, usually announced on a loudspeaker, can cause problems for the hard of hearing person. Commuter flights pose an additional problem because several flights leave from one gate and you must constantly be on the alert for changes. Gate personnel don't always remember that you have told them that you do not hear well and to alert you to important messages. One way to keep informed is to ask a fellow traveler on the same flight to inform you of such announcements.

On the airplane, hearing the safety and evacuation procedures, the menu options, and announcements by the pilot can be difficult. Giving a written note to the flight attendant with your name and seat number is one way to solve this problem. You also can ask your seatmate to alert you if any unexpected announcements are made. If you do not hear well, you are not supposed to sit in the exit rows where you would be responsible for evacuation procedures in case of emergency.

The FAA fact sheet "Air Travel by People with Disabilities" addresses questions and concerns about the travel of persons with disabilities in airports and via airplanes in the aftermath of the terrorist attacks on September 11, 2001. It can be found on-line at www.faa.gov/acr/AT-PWD.doc. In addition, please see these two fact sheets:

- "Steps Taken to Ensure New Security Requirements Preserve and Respect the Civil Rights of People with Disabilities," available from airconsumer.ost.dot.gov/airconsumer/rules/20011029.htm
- "Facts for Air Travelers . . . from the Aviation Consumer Protection Division: Passengers with Disabilities," available from www.dot.gov/airconsumer/disabled.htm

FAA regulations allow passengers to carry assistive listening devices in their carry-on luggage. Be prepared to explain to security personnel how ALDs are used. Whether you can or cannot hear announcements, remember to turn off FM equipment during take-off and landing because it interferes with the radio transmission between tower and cockpit.

People with hearing loss often experience a feeling of full-ness or blockage when flying. This blockage of the ear, *barotitis*, which is caused by changes in atmospheric pres-sure, is both mild and reversible. The best thing you can do to avoid it is to not fly when you have a cold or an upper respiratory allergic reaction. If you must fly under either of these conditions, or you know that your ears get blocked when flying, take a decongestant nasal spray with you and spray your nose two or three times, one or two hours before landing.

If your ears start to feel blocked during landing, swallow repeatedly, sip some fluid, or hold your nose and try to "pop" your ears by blowing out gently while your mouth and nose are closed. If you have significant pain or hearing loss after landing, see your ear doctor.

Bon voyage!

(35)

Hearing in the Courtroom

What would you do if you received a summons to re-port for jury duty? You might take the easy way out and use your hearing loss as an excuse for not serving: *"If I can't hear the proceedings or the discussion among jurors, I will be violating the rights of the litigants; therefore, I can't serve."* On the other hand, you might see jury service as a duty and a right to participate in our legal system. When you can't serve, you are denied equal access to our justice system.

If you are an advocate for the rights of hard of hearing people, you also may view jury duty as an opportunity to ensure that the courts are in compliance with the ADA (see chapter 29). Most courthouses have installed ramps for people who need them and hired sign language interpreters for people who are deaf, but often they have no assistive listening devices to accommodate people who are hard of hearing.

Many court systems employ voice mail as the means for responding to the summons. This often is a difficult option for people with hearing loss. Although you can get a family member or friend to help you understand the message if you do not hear well on the telephone, or use the relay service, consider suggesting another method of responding to the commissioner of jurors, such as a return postcard.

Your response to the request to serve should include a statement such as: "I can serve if the facility has assistive listening systems, communication access realtime translation (CART) (see page 64), or devices in place to accommodate people who are hard of hearing." You also will need to state your specific needs.

At the courthouse, you may see signs posted outside a courtroom that indicate assistive listening devices are available. This does not mean that they are in every room of the courthouse or that they are in working condition. Very often, only one person in the court system is familiar with the devices—where they are kept, how they function, how to maintain them—and may not be available the day you are on jury duty. You may have to use your assertive skills to ensure that the system works for you before the proceedings begin. You must let them know what you need with ample notice.

The National Court Reporters Association works continuously to develop and implement innovative communication solutions in order to provide courtroom accessibility for every litigant, judge, juror, lawyer, and spectator. Court reporters use CART, the instant transcription of the spoken word into English text, using a stenotype machine, notebook computer, and realtime software, to facilitate participation in judicial proceedings. With this technology, the message can be displayed on a video monitor, printed out as a rough transcript, captured on a floppy disk or CD, or printed in Braille seconds after information is transmitted by the court reporter to the computer. Using the skills of court reporters, CART is specifically recognized by the Americans with Disabilities Act as an assistive technology that affords effective communication and has become an accepted and desired tool in the courtroom.

At the same time you are ensuring that the courtroom is accessible, it is equally important that the jury deliberation room and other hearing rooms also are accessible. For a fair and impartial trial, you need to be privy to all communication.

Serving in Other Capacities

If you are a litigant or a witness in a trial, it is equally important for you to hear the proceedings. This is not the time to deny or hide your hearing loss; it is the time to speak up for what you need to serve the system well.

Officers of the Court

Attorneys, clerks, and judges also may experience hearing loss. In order to serve the judicial system, it is important to hear the proceedings. As a responsible officer of the court, you know that this is not the time to hide a hearing loss. This is the time to take a leadership role by ensuring that the courtroom is accessible to you and to other people with hearing loss. Explore the options available to ensure a fair trial.

Other Legal Situations

It is essential that you understand what is being communicated during all legal proceedings, including appearances in small claims court, observing a trial, and during everyday legal procedures such as preparing a will, settling an estate, conducting real estate transactions, resolving civil disputes, and preparing tax forms. Be sure to explain to your lawyer and others involved that you have a hearing loss and how they can best communicate with you.

This last advice applies outside the lawyer's office as well. It includes being upfront about your hearing loss in discussions with Social Security and other government-agency personnel, or when being questioned by police officers and public officials.

(36)

Volunteering or Returning to Work

MANY PEOPLE who retire from the work force often decide to return to work part time or to engage in volunteer work. Your hearing loss should not deter you from either.

In the past, popular misconceptions about hearing loss were pervasive and strongly influenced decisions about whether firms and volunteer organizations recruited and hired hard of hearing people. Today, however, public attention to the nature and consequences of hearing loss never has been at a higher level.

The Americans with Disabilities Act specifies that employers cannot discriminate against qualified individuals with disabilities who, with reasonable accommodations, can perform essential functions of the position. Reasonable accommodations for hard of hearing people—such as accessible telephones, assistive devices in meeting rooms, job restructuring, and safety alerts—are relatively inexpensive and can enable you to do a job.

Remember that your previous training, background, and skills are more important than your hearing loss. Focus on what you can do, not on what might cause problems.

A number of practical strategies can help you overcome anxiety and get the work or volunteer position you want. The key to coping with hearing loss in the workplace is to be open about your hearing loss and let others know how best to communicate with you so you may achieve your highest potential and contribute your talent.

Employers and volunteer organizations may have little experience working with people with hearing loss. Even though you may be nervous, being open and honest about your hearing loss may help to enhance others' comfort level and ensure a smooth interview.

The interview presents an opportunity to show that although you have a hearing loss, you can still function well and do the job. This is no time to hide your hearing loss. If you need assistive devices and own them, take them with you. If you need assistive devices that you do not own but are necessary for you to function effectively on the job, you should request them up front so that your communication needs with employer or volunteer agency are clear from the beginning.

Once you are hired or accepted for a volunteer position, demonstrate your commitment by the quality and quantity of the work you perform and your work ethic.

In order to ensure that you have understood what you are supposed to do on the job, confirm instructions after they are given. You might ask for instructions in writing if this is more comfortable for you.

Often, meetings, training sessions, and small conferences are situations in which it is difficult to hear. Do something about this early on. Unresolved communication difficulties, whether with co-workers, other volunteers, supervisors, or clients, can make you look inefficient and incapable of carrying out your responsibilities.

Vocational Rehabilitation

You may wish to investigate your eligibility for vocational rehabilitation (VR) services. VR is the nationwide federal/state program that helps people with disabilities obtain appropriate training so that they can secure employment. All states, territories, and trust areas have a vocational rehabilitation agency. To be eligible for VR services, you must, among other requirements, have a physical or mental impairment that is a substantial impediment to employment.

The Corporation for National and Community Service

If you are looking for a satisfying avenue for connecting to the outside world, the Corporation for National and Community Service (CNCS) provides opportunities for people of all ages and backgrounds, including those with hearing loss, to participate in community and national service programs. Through its three streams of service—AmeriCorps, the Senior Corps, and Learn and Serve America—CNCS provides meaningful opportunities to meet important needs in the community and the United States. Successful participation in CNCS programs also provides educational awards or stipends. For information on how to contact CNCS, see appendix A.

(37)

A New Friend: The Internet

Hearing aids, assistive devices, coping strategies, and healthy living are at the top of the list for people with hearing loss. There is, however, another device you may not have considered, but one that can help you communicate easily and bring the world to your doorstep: a personal computer (PC) with a program that gives you access to the Internet and electronic mail (e-mail). Computers can be the answer to many of the communication difficulties you encounter daily as a person who is hard of hearing.

If you already have embraced computers, you are on the way to having another means of communicating easily with family members, friends, banks, airlines, and businesses, to name a few. The world is at your fingertips.

You may argue, "I don't even know how to type." You are never too old to learn, and hunting and pecking, although slower than ten-finger typing—the new word is *keyboarding*, by the way—enables you to become computer literate while picking up speed.

You may be hesitant, however. "Computers are expensive," you might say. They are—but well worth the investment when you realize all that you can do to facilitate communication. The new Net PCs cost less, and a used rebuilt computer is another alternative.

Some people with hearing loss find TV–Internet connections helpful. Several companies, including AOL and Microsoft, package hardware and provide interactive television services that can be used with a television monitor for e-mail and web browsing.

You might also consider using a Personal Digital Assistant (PDA). These small hand-held computers have multiple functions such as a calendar, address book, notepad, and sometimes e-mail and a web browser. Most can communicate with other devices, either via hardware or wirelessly. Relatively few of the PDAs have vibrating or visual alerts, but the more expensive ones are more likely to have them.

Another way to communicate is to use a text paging system with audible or vibration notification. In addition, a few digital cell phones are hearing aid compatible and are useful for being alerted to emergencies because they can receive short text messages.

Ways to Use Your Computer

You may ask, "What can I do with a computer that I can't do with my old typewriter?" You can write personal and business letters or prepare newsletters and organize presentations for your volunteer work, all the tasks for which you use a typewriter, but you can do these with less frustration and you can do so many other things.

- A most valuable use of the computer for older Americans is keeping in touch with family and friends. When the telephone becomes a barrier to good communication because you are asking the person on the other end of the line to repeat, or when you are having difficulty understanding the voices of grandchildren and you want to say the right thing in order to keep your relationship with them meaningful, a computer and an e-mail program could be the answer.

- Although hearing the voices of family members and being able to discern their moods from the tone is certainly a preferred way to communicate, e-mail provides a new world for people with hearing loss. It also keeps you from playing telephone tag. When you can leave a message with someone who has the information you need and receive an answer in writing, why spend time calling and struggling to hear the answer?

- If you use a TTY and would like to communicate with friends who have computers or if you use a computer and would like to communicate with friends who use a TTY, you might consider a computer with special equipment that allows it to function as a TTY. This feature may add to the cost, but if staying in touch is a priority for you, spend the money.

- You may be able to equip your computer with a special modem—a device that allows your computer to use telephone lines to transmit information to other computers or terminals equipped with compatible modems—to make it function as a TTY.

- The Internet also will provide you with an opportunity to participate in discussion groups and chat rooms, a new way of gaining and sharing information, making new friends with similar interests, and socializing.
- You can track your finances, and even do your banking and check writing. You can get the latest stock market information, track your investments, and buy and sell.
- If you enjoy games, a wealth of software is available in this area. If you are interested in genealogy, programs exist that make the organizing of information easy.
- If travel is high on your priority list, the Internet provides extensive information about places to visit, what there is to see, hotels and motels, and how best to get there. Airline scheduling, booking tickets, and finding reduced rates—all are at your fingertips.
- If you have arthritis in addition to your hearing loss, and find that writing is painful, a computer keyboard may relieve the stress of corresponding with loved ones or for business purposes.
- And if you are interested in returning to work or finding a part-time position, computer skills combined with your other skills and experience, could put you back in the workplace with a new career.

A word of warning. The technology in the field of computers is burgeoning and changes daily. The day you buy a computer, it will be out of date. But don't let that keep you from considering one—it can keep you connected, informed, and in touch with the world.

If you already own a computer and can access the World Wide Web, find out the latest information about hearing loss by visiting http://www.shhh.org.

(38)

Hearing Loss and Eldercare

WITH PEOPLE living longer, many of them with multiple disabilities, the need for eldercare is expected to increase. Because fewer potential family members will be available to serve as caregivers for those needing long-term care, the demand for the services provided by nursing homes and adult day-care centers is expected to escalate.

If someone you know has a hearing loss and is living in a nursing home, your role as a friend or relative is essential. You can provide a valuable service by becoming an advocate. Nursing home residents have rights and responsibilities, and unless they are in a nonresponsive state, they should be informed about their medical treatment and decisions related to their health problems. When residents don't understand what is happening, their apprehension rises to abnormal proportions.

People who lose their hearing late in life concomitant with the aging process are extremely sensitive and vulnerable to the denial syndrome for they view hearing loss as tangible evidence of aging or decline.

For some older people who are living in nursing homes, hearing loss may have contributed to their placement in a long-term care facility. Communication problems such as inappropriate answers or apparent lack of response may be mistaken for mental confusion or loss of mental acuity.

Communication between staff members and residents who have a hearing loss takes time and effort and often is a low priority. Since nursing homes are usually short staffed, residents with hearing loss often experience subtle, imagined, and even blatant discrimination for a variety of reasons ranging from lack of understanding on the part of staff members, misdiagnosis, or sheer lack of staff time for special efforts to communicate effectively, to impatience with the resident's refusal to admit a hearing problem.

Individuals who approach old age with negative feelings and at the same time have to deal with a progressive hearing loss are ill-equipped with coping skills for handling the accompanying prejudice/discrimination or for understanding the thoughtless stigmatization even among their peers.

Nursing homes would do well to become knowledgeable about the psychosocial effects of hearing loss on the individual (see chapter 39). By recognizing that an isolating hearing loss—alone or in combination with other health problems such as diminished vision, manual dexterity, and memory loss—can increase a resident's anxiety, dependency, frustration, confusion, suspicion, and depression.

Providing Information

The following simple but relevant pieces of information you provide to nursing home staff members can greatly improve the comfort, adjustment, and mental health of the resident with hearing loss.

1. Ensure that the staff members know that the resident is hard of hearing. Educate them. Tell them how to communicate by giving them specific strategies such as "try to get the resident's attention before speaking" and "it is often helpful to flick the light switch on and off to alert the resident that someone is entering the room."

You may need to repeat this information because staff members may forget, and you may be communicating with different personnel on different shifts. Be patient and polite, but be persistent.

2. Alert staff members to the fact that the resident does not understand messages over the intercom. Ask that information specific for the resident be delivered face to face. You might suggest that a note or the access symbol be posted at the nurses' station as a reminder when communicating important general information. Remind staff members that even though people with hearing loss use their eyes to make up for what they cannot hear, most people who lose their hearing later in life are not skilled speechreaders, and only 30 to 40 percent of speech is visible on the lips.

3. Residents who have difficulty understanding conversation or instructions, ask for frequent repetition, turn the radio or television on too loud, can't understand when on the telephone, and cup a hand to the ear may be experiencing additional hearing loss. You can remind the staff to check for a buildup of earwax and have it removed. If hearing does not improve, you can suggest that a hearing evaluation may be in order. Many nursing homes have a consulting audiologist who is available on call to evaluate hearing loss and hearing aids.

4. If the resident wears a hearing aid, you can ensure that it is in proper working order and that an adequate supply of batteries is on hand. You might instruct staff members that a daily check of the hearing aid should be as much a part of the morning and bedtime patient care as the cleaning of dentures and washing of eyeglasses. Staff members should know how to turn the aid on and

off, set the volume control, and replace weak or dead
batteries.

5. For some residents who do not or will not use a hearing
   aid, a one-on-one communicator can serve as a primary
   amplification device. They can ease the chore of conversing with residents who have a moderate or severe
   hearing loss (see chapter 18).

Many of the recommended procedures for a hospital stay
discussed in chapter 33 also apply to nursing home residency.

(39)

Overcoming Psychosocial Effects of Hearing Loss

THE LOSS, even partial, of the sense of hearing, upon
which much of the hearing community's interpersonal communication is based, can be described as a major life loss. It
is much different from hearing loss that is present at birth or
begins in early childhood, particularly from a psychosocial
perspective, because it can cause changes in your job, mar-
riage, and entire lifestyle. When you lose your hearing in
adulthood, you experience a kind of deprivation, the loss of
a sense you have always taken for granted. The multidimen-
sional effects of that loss can alter the way you feel about
yourself as well as the way you think others feel about you.

Your personality does not change because you lose your
hearing. People who are naturally quiet and reserved may

experience their hearing loss quite differently than those who are friendly and outgoing by nature. Because you are unique, you will experience hearing loss in your own way; however, some predictable behaviors are common to people who experience the onset of hearing loss as adults. It helps to understand those behaviors because they validate many of the feelings you have about yourself and about how other people react and respond to you. Understanding can also motivate you to help yourself develop coping strategies that work.

Hearing loss may create a communication barrier between you and other people. Spontaneity in conversation may become difficult because your brain needs to work overtime to process information and fill in the missing pieces of the conversation puzzle. Your ability to cope with these changes will affect the way your hearing loss affects your life from a psychosocial perspective.

Perceptions

Your self-image and the image you convey to others are based heavily on perceptions, but sometimes perceptions do not reflect reality. For example, you may believe that only old people wear hearing aids, that hearing loss is a sign of old age. That belief alone may prevent you from admitting you have a hearing loss. Other people may have perceptions about you that portray you very differently from the person you really are. If you do not respond to other people when or as expected, they will form perceptions that define the way they think about you. If you conceal your hearing loss, there is nothing to indicate those perceptions are wrong. People will define you by their faulty perceptions rather than by reality. They may even choose not to acknowledge you in the future because they believe you chose to be unfriendly to them in the past. This kind of seesaw can create hurt feelings for everyone. Hard of hearing people often feel that "nobody understands" them, which may be partially true but is all too often interpreted as "nobody likes me." This belief can lead to mild and even more serious levels of depression.

Denial

If you refuse to admit you cannot hear well and persist in blaming other people for not speaking clearly or loudly enough, you are in a psychological state known as denial. When you are in denial you cannot seek help for your hearing loss; in fact, you become quite helpless. When you choose this negative coping strategy, you will fool no one but yourself. If the people who know you don't guess that you have a hearing problem, they will wonder why you act or react strangely. People whom you meet for the first time may perceive you as aloof, dull, or even mentally inferior. Their conclusions about your unusual behavior have the potential to be far more damaging than the upfront knowledge that you simply don't hear well.

Avoidance

As time passes, you may find yourself avoiding situations in which hearing is difficult, as well as certain people whose voices you know you have difficulty understanding. Avoidance is a negative coping strategy that will gradually erode your ties to both people and activities that you formerly enjoyed. Avoidance leads to different degrees of withdrawal from your former way of life—on the job, with friends, and in leisure activities—and within your immediate family. In fact, you can effectively isolate yourself from the many joys of parenting and grandparenting if you choose to avoid having to listen to your younger family members who have higher-pitched (and more difficult to understand) voices, rather than getting help for your hearing.

The reasons for denial run the gamut from negative cultural attitudes to ignorance about the nature of hearing loss itself. You deny because you don't understand the physiology of hearing loss. Because you are confused you cannot possibly tell other people how to help you. When denial becomes chronic and long lasting, your hearing problem will intensify because it becomes a problem for everyone. If you become angry and defiant when the subject of hearing loss is brought up, you will create a standoff that nobody can win. Others become frustrated and may even go so far as to begin avoiding you.

Self-imposed isolation that eventually results from denial can lead to loneliness. But it is not necessary to live a lonely life if you admit you have a hearing loss and do whatever you need to do to help yourself hear better. If your associates believe you could help yourself but choose not to, they may lose patience with you. On the other hand, you will find that most people will go out of their way to learn effective communication strategies if they know you are helping yourself as best you can.

Other Negative Behaviors

You learned the difference between aggressive, assertive, and passive communication in chapter 24.

- Aggressiveness is a common reaction to the frustrations caused by hearing loss, but an aggressive person makes demands that cross boundaries and interfere with the rights of other people. For example, if you insist on having the television at your preferred loudness level rather than using one of the many assistive devices that enable you to control the volume without creating an environment that is too loud for everyone else, you are exhibiting aggressive controlling behavior.

- Monopolizing is another example of aggressive behavior. This behavior is more common among people who have always been gregarious and outgoing. The monopolizer controls conversations by dominating them. The logic is simple: If you do all the talking, you won't have to listen; therefore, you will know what is being discussed. Needless to say, this behavior will become tiresome for others. Your associates may cope with this behavior by avoiding you.

- Passive behavior can be as devastating as aggressive behavior. Passive people do not complain nor do they seek help; they simply accept the hearing loss as a fact of life. The psychosocial implications of passive behavior vary depending on the innate personality of the individual.

- Assertiveness is the middle ground between aggressiveness and passivity. When you are assertive, you learn how to help yourself as well as to help other people help you. You may learn to find some humor in the mistakes you make. You also accept the reality that you will, on occasion, experience feelings of being "left out" of conversations and decision making. These times will still be hurtful, but you learn not to let your feelings interfere with your personal interactions with others. How you assert yourself when this happens will have a direct bearing on the cooperation you receive from others.

Fear

Considerable fear may be attached to hearing loss. Fear may arise because you become concerned about how your hearing loss is going to affect your way of life. If you are employed, the fear of losing your job may be extremely stressful. Hard of hearing people are constantly faced with the fear of misunderstanding and misinterpreting incoming information. Fear can lead to chronic worry and anxiety.

Fear is the emotion that is biologically designed to elicit the human body's stress response. The stress response, often called the "fight or flight response," is biologically designed to help you fight off or run away from the impending danger of a life-threatening situation. Rarely does hearing loss create a life-threatening situation, yet many hard of hearing people live in an unhealthy state of chronic stress because they feel constantly threatened. Learning effective methods of managing stress should be one of your personal goals (see chapter 40).

Self-Help

Self-help combines accepting your hearing loss and using appropriate technology along with a willingness to become educated about the causes of and potential strategies for living with hearing loss. Self-help may mean being fitted with a hearing aid and learning the basics of speechreading. It could mean that you use assistive devices that go beyond your hearing aid. It may mean learning cued speech or some other form of manual communication. The myriad options available to you can make a positive difference when you open your mind to learning about them and adapting them to your needs.

(40)
Healthy Living/Managing Stress

ALL PEOPLE experience good and bad stress. At its best, stress serves to invigorate, motivate, and give you the personal power and strength to achieve and excel. At its worst, stress will cause the systems within your body to chronically overwork. Stress becomes a concern when it is chronic and poorly managed.

By now you know that hearing loss can be stressful. You also know that your physical and emotional well-being depends on how you learn to manage the hearing loss and stress in your life. When your body's stress response is triggered, several physical reactions take place, including increased cardiac output, breathing, and blood pressure. You may feel your heart pound and experience shortness of breath. Under stress, your muscles will tense because blood flows to them to provide you with extra physical strength. These bodily responses are obvious to you. All of these normal responses are intended to help you face situations that are potentially life threatening. This is why the stress response is often called the "fight or flight response."

Your bodily responses to negative stress create symptoms. When your muscles tense up you may experience pain, most often in the shoulders, neck, and legs. Most headache pain is the result of muscle tension. Your digestive tract may react with constipation, diarrhea, or pain from spasms. Because your breathing rate increases you may perspire and experience dry mouth. The stress response creates different

141

symptoms in different people. Take a moment to think about what happens to your body and mind when you feel stressed or fearful. You will recognize the effects as you personally experience them.

Stressors

The stress response kicks in when a demand, situation (real or perceived), or circumstance disrupts your normal state of equilibrium. Whatever elicits the stress response is called a *stressor*. Stressors may be perceived rather than real. Worry is a huge stressor for most people. If you spend time worrying about situations that may or may not occur because you are afraid of how you will cope with your hearing loss if they happen, you are dealing with a perceived stressor. It's much like worrying for days ahead about a trip to the dentist. The real event is far less traumatic than the perceived and imagined event that caused you to worry and feel stressed for days. It is not healthy to expend time and energy with the stressor called *worry*. In fact, it can actually do harm if you don't learn to control it.

Stress Management

A successful stress management program will require a two-pronged approach that includes both stress prevention and stress management. You will want to adopt a holistic approach that incorporates relaxation strategies, time management, good nutrition, exercise, and a drug-free lifestyle, all of which are vital components of an effective stress management program. When you minimize the amount of stress in your life and the effects of stress on your body, you will discover that you can also manage your hearing loss well.

Time Management

Time management is a key to stress management. Schedule time for work and play by balancing the daily routine. Recreational activities that you enjoy can serve as a great source of stress release. Don't overprogram yourself, but don't use your hearing loss as an excuse to say no when you really should say yes. Rest and relaxation should be important parts of your schedule. If you enjoy volunteer work be sure to include it in your schedule.

Good Nutrition

Diet and lifestyle have an indirect effect on hearing loss. Both hearing loss and tinnitus typically become temporarily worse when one is fatigued, under stress, and malnourished. Although these changes are transient, their effects may influence your general sense of well-being. As with any medical problem, the better your diet, the more adequate your rest, and the better your sense of well-being, the less effect the hearing loss will have on you.

- *Low salt.*When you reduce fluid retention in your body you also reduce the fluid in your inner ear. The buildup of fluid associated with tinnitus and Ménière's disease can be reduced with appropriate control of salt in your diet.
- *Low fat.* If you have hyperlipidemia (excessive amounts of fat and fatty substances in the blood), you also may have inner ear symptoms such as tinnitus, dizziness, and fullness in the ears. By following a dietary regime to reduce or eliminate the cardiovascular risk factors, the inner ear symptoms may also diminish or disappear.
- *No caffeine.* For many people caffeine can be a stimulant. If you are experiencing stress, you may want to cut back

on your intake. Remember, caffeine is present not only in coffee and tea, but in soft drinks and chocolate as well.

Medications

Drugs often are prescribed to relieve stress, but they do not relieve the underlying cause; they can even create more stress. If you take several medications—over the counter and those prescribed for you—try to get all your medications through one doctor, your internist preferably. Many medications are ototoxic and combinations can cause other problems (see chapter 8).

Exercise

Whether you engage in an activity as easy as walking or something more strenuous, physical exercise can relieve tension and relax you. Exercise also increases blood flow to the ears, which is known to improve hearing. Breathing, a relaxation technique described below, is often considered the number one exercise.

Relaxation

When your body is chronically stressed, it experiences continuous wear and tear with little or no rest. It doesn't take a great deal of physiological knowledge to understand why it is not healthy to allow your body to remain in a stressed state for long periods of time. Therefore, it is very important for you to learn how to allow your body to return to its normal level of functioning which is called *homeostasis*. To do this, you must learn to elicit your body's natural stress fighting mechanism, the relaxation response.

Relaxation is the exact opposite of stress. Your body cannot be relaxed and stressed at the same time. Relaxation, which begins with proper breathing, is the key to managing stress. For most people today, true relaxation is a learned skill rather than a natural one.

You may remember learning about diaphragmatic breathing when you were a child in grade school. You probably even practiced it then. Most likely you have forgotten all about the rudiments of proper breathing; now you either do it naturally or you do not. In fact, you may not even be able to describe the way you breathe even when you think about it. Proper breathing can be visualized. Picture your lungs as a glass and your breath as water. When water is poured into a glass it fills from the bottom up. When water goes out of the glass it empties from the top down. That is exactly how proper breathing works. Experiment by visualizing it that way.

The breathing cycle has three phases: inhalation, pause, and exhalation. The inhalation phase is the tension-producing phase. As you awaken from sleep or a relaxed state, it is normal to yawn, stretch, and take a deep breath simultaneously. The muscular tension created produces a feeling of invigoration, refreshment, mental stimulation, and alertness. When you practice relaxation techniques, you will use the inhalation phase to bring yourself out of a relaxed state.

The exhalation phase of the breathing cycle is the relaxation phase. During exhalation you let go of the tension that developed naturally in the body from inhalation. The exhalation phase is the built-in mechanism for relaxation that everyone has. Exhalation normally is felt as a downward movement because the muscles relax and gravity causes you to sink down. The sensations identified with exhalation—feelings of heaviness, slowing down, letting go, comfort, and contentment—are exactly opposite of the sensations of inhalation. These sensations can be easily identified and sensed. When practicing relaxation techniques, you will concentrate on the exhalation phase and disregard the inhalation phase. Begin your relaxation program now by concentrating on your breathing rhythm. Practice this for a few minutes several times during the day. You should not fall asleep during this exercise. Remember to bring yourself out of the relaxed state by inhaling deeply and stretching. When you are breathing properly, you will feel refreshed after only a few minutes of practicing this exercise. Try it the next time you are faced with a stressor.

Once you have mastered the release of tension through proper breathing you will want to learn about other stress management techniques such as progressive relaxation, total body relaxation, and imaging. Your local library has many books that will provide you with step-by-step instructions on how to master these techniques. You may even find a class through a local health center that offers instruction in relaxation. One word of caution for people with hearing loss: Relaxation works best when you are comfortable closing your eyes. If you need to speechread a group leader, you may find the group setting uncomfortable, even stressful. Be sure the group leader understands your needs. Better yet, find a relaxation program especially designed for hard of hearing people. Self Help for Hard of Hearing People often includes such a session in the annual convention programming. Participants then take the information home to share with other hard of hearing people.

(41)

What Is SHHH?

SELF HELP for Hard of Hearing People (SHHH) is a non-profit educational organization dedicated to the well being of people of all ages and communication styles who do not hear well. The primary purpose of SHHH is to open the world of communication to people with hearing loss by providing information, education, advocacy, and support.

The SHHH headquarters in Bethesda, Maryland, provides information and education on many aspects of hearing loss—from technological and medical advances to coping and parenting strategies—through publications, resource materials, and an annual convention that offers workshops and opportunities to try out new technology.

SHHH's award-winning bimonthly magazine, *Hearing Loss: The Journal of Self Help for Hard of Hearing People,* has a readership of 200,000 and is the only educational journal for hard of hearing people in America. The unwritten theme of "Hearing Loss: You Can Do Something about It" permeates the pages of each issue. Authors are people of various backgrounds—renowned professionals in the hearing health industry, psychologists, doctors, scientists, and educators. Other popular articles are personal narratives written by SHHH members.

SHHH's knowledgeable staff members represent the interests of people with hearing loss, and advocate for full access to services for them in government, professional, academic, private sector, and research forums. SHHH supports medical research, new technology, and legislation that will alleviate the effects of hearing loss. Together with its members, the organization worked toward the passage of the Americans with Disabilities Act, developed guidelines relating to hearing access, and continues to encourage provision of appropriate accommodations at the local level.

SHHH and its members believe that people with hearing loss can help themselves and one another to participate fully and successfully in society. They recognize that in order to remain in control of their lives, people with hearing loss must first educate themselves, and then their families, friends, co-workers, teachers, hearing health care providers, people in industry and government, and others with whom they interact. SHHH philosophy emphasizes that informed consumers make better decisions about the options available to them and are able to address hearing loss more effectively than people who do not have such information available.

A yearly convention held in locations nationwide provides educational programs designed to provide information that best meets members' needs, regardless of where they are in the process of learning to live with hearing loss. A good mix of topics for newcomers and oldtimers alike ranges from the latest in hearing aids and assistive technology, to coping strategies, employment, and parenting. The exhibitors in the exhibit hall, which houses the largest displays of information, services, and assistive technology for hard of hearing consumers in the country, spend hours demonstrating, answering questions, and listening to participants' needs, while they have numerous opportunities for hands-on experience.

In addition to the national headquarters, SHHH has thirteen state organizations that have been established since 1992. Nine are associations with elected officers and four are state offices with an appointed director and a core group of volunteers. They are located in California, Florida, Georgia, Michigan, Minnesota, New Jersey, New York, North Carolina, Oregon, Pennsylvania, Texas, Washington, and Wisconsin. All are extensions of the national office and are carrying out the mission of SHHH in the states. The state organizations are credible resources within the state, working alongside other state agencies and organizations to represent people with hearing loss; improve services; provide information, referral, education, and training; and collectively advocate for enhanced communication in the state.

SHHH has 250 chapters nationwide whose participants meet regularly to learn about hearing loss from one another as well as from professionals in the field. Local chapters emphasize that with education, information, shared experience, and support, people with hearing loss can develop strategies for living successfully. Chapter participants also advocate for access in the workplace, hotels, schools, court systems, and medical and entertainment facilities in order to help make their communities and states more accessible for people with hearing loss. Local SHHH meetings offer:

- A place where your hearing loss is accepted and understood
- A communication-accessible stress-free environment
- An opportunity to share your concerns and learn from others
- Ways in which you can make a difference for yourself and others
- Support, referrals, and information
- Coping strategies and the latest technological information
- Enlightenment for family members, relatives, and friends

• Fellowship and friendship—listening ears and helping hands

If you would like to participate in an SHHH chapter or start a new one, contact the SHHH chapter development office. To find a chapter where you live, call SHHH and inquire.

For more information about membership, annual conventions, SHHH chapters, the bookstore, and programs, contact:

Self Help for Hard of Hearing People
7910 Woodmont Avenue, Suite 1200
Bethesda, MD 20814
(301) 657-2248 (Voice)
(301) 657-2249 (TTY)
Fax: (301) 913-9413
Web: http://www.shhh.org

(42)

Some Final Words

OVER THE thirty years that I have lived with hearing loss, I have learned a few lessons:

• Hearing loss can cause frustration; however, with education and proper attitude, the frustration and the disability can be lessened.
• Responsive and experienced hearing health care providers are worth their weight in gold.

- Support groups are essential.
- Family members, friends, and co-workers can provide a large measure of support, but they need to be educated to your needs and you to theirs.
- The market is full of assistive devices that should be explored and used.
- The technology used in hearing aids and assistive devices is burgeoning and improving.

The Importance of Communication

We all need to communicate effectively. In order to do this, I have a few suggestions:

- Learn as much as possible about your own hearing loss.
- Learn what services are best provided by otolaryngologists, audiologists, and hearing aid specialists, and choose the professional who best provides the service you need.
- Together with your hearing health care specialist, evaluate hearing aids and get the one—two if recommended—that best meets your needs.
- Learn assertive techniques to use with family members and other people, such as "It would help me to understand you, if you faced me when you spoke" and "I can be a part of this conversation if only one of you speaks at a time."
- Find other sources of support, as well. It is important to meet other people with similar hearing losses, and these people may be found through membership in groups such as SHHH.
- Learn some basic sign language; if nothing else, learn the alphabet. On my first trip abroad after I lost my

hearing, I taught my daughter to fingerspell the alphabet. She then could help me with foreign names when I was having difficulty understanding them.

- Find out which assistive listening and alerting devices can help you in various situations. Keep abreast of the latest technology, since it changes rapidly.
- Keep your expectations for improvement realistic.
- And more important than everything else, keep your sense of humor.

Glossary

ABR. For *Auditory Brainstem Response Audiometry*. A hearing test in which a person's ability to hear "clicks" is determined by comparing a resting brain wave pattern with a brain waving pattern when "clicks" are made.

Americans with Disabilities Act (ADA). Public Law 101-336 passed in 1990 that prohibits discrimination on the basis of disability in employment, transportation, public accommodation, state and local government, and telecommunications.

adventitiously deaf. People who were born hearing and who lost their hearing later in life.

alerting device. A visual or tactile device that alerts a person who cannot hear to sounds such as door knocks, telephone rings, and fire alarms.

American Sign Language (ASL). *See* sign language.

amplified telephone. A telephone that is equipped with volume control either built into the handset, the body of the telephone, or via an attachment.

assistive listening device (ALD). A device that, used with or without a hearing aid, brings a speaker's voice directly to the ear of the person with hearing loss.

assistive listening system (ALS). A system used in rooms of assembly and with large groups to make dialogue accessible. *See also* audio induction loop, infrared, and FM.

audiogram. A graph on which a person's ability to hear different pitches of sound is recorded.

audiologist. A specialist in testing and evaluating hearing and providing nonmedical management of hearing loss, including hearing aids, assistive devices, and rehabilitation.

audio induction loop. A coil of electrical wire that creates a magnetic field that can transmit sound and thus permit individuals with hearing loss to hear the sound without background noise or echoes.

audiometer. A device for testing hearing.

aural rehabilitation. Specialized training for people with hearing loss that includes speechreading, how to listen, how to speak.

Automatic Speech Recognition (ASR). A computer system that converts the spoken word into text.

binaural. Refers to hearing with both ears.

body aid. A powerful hearing aid that is worn on the body and is connected to an earmold by a cord.

BTE (behind-the-ear) aid. A hearing aid worn behind the ear that is connected to an earmold by thin plastic tubing.

canal aid. *See* ITC (in-the-canal) aid.

CAN. For *computer-assisted notetaking.*

CART. For *communication access realtime translation.* A system that allows the instant conversion of the spoken word into English text, using a stenotype machine, notebook computer, and realtime software.

cerumen. Earwax.

closed captions. Text of spoken dialogue and sounds displayed on TV and videos that is visible only to people using a caption decoder or TV with built-in decoder chip.

cochlear implant. A surgically implanted electronic device that allows people with profound hearing loss to hear environmental sounds, improve speechreading, monitor their own speech, and often understand voices.

conductive hearing loss. A hearing loss caused by damage to the outer or middle ear. This type of hearing loss often is correctable medically or surgically.

congenitally deaf. Said of people who are born deaf or become deaf soon after birth.

C-Print. A computer-aided speech-to-print transcription system.

CROS. For *Contralateral Routing of Signal.* A type of hearing aid often recommended when one ear has nearly normal hearing.

Cued Speech. A sound-based visual communication system that uses eight handshapes in four different locations (cues) in combination with the natural mouth movements of speech.

DAI. *See* direct audio input.

deaf. A term that may be used to describe a person with severe or profound hearing loss.

decibel (dB). The unit used to measure the intensity or loudness of sound; the higher the dB, the louder the sound.

decoder. An electronic device that reads a special code in the television signal and converts it to characters on the viewer's television screen.

direct audio input. An option that bypasses the hearing aid's microphone by plugging a sound source directly into a hearing aid.

earbud. A small transducer encased in a round foam rubber covering that is inserted in the ear canal. Like earphones, earbuds deliver sound to the ear, but many people think they are more comfortable than earphones.

earmold. An acrylic or polyvinyl mold that couples the sound from the hearing aid to the ear.

e-mail. Electronic mail, where messages are sent and received electronically; used by many computer owners.

feedback. The squealing noise emitted when some of the amplified sound escapes from around an earmold or ITE and ITC hearing aids.

fingerspelling. Using handshapes to represent the letters of the alphabet.

frequency. The number of vibrations per second, or pitch, of a sound, usually expressed in Hz (hertz). The lower the Hz, the lower the pitch.

FM (Frequency Modulation) system. A device that transmits amplified sound by radio waves to a receiver, thus eliminating background noise and distance problems.

hard of hearing. A term that may be used to describe a person with any degree of hearing loss, ranging from mild to profound, who can understand some speech sounds with or without a hearing aid.

hearing aid. An electronic device used to amplify sound. *See* BTE, ITC, ITE.

Hearing Aid Compatibility Act of 1988. Act that mandates that all telephones manufactured in the United States from 1989 on should be hearing aid-compatible.

hearing dog. A dog that has completed a training course to alert its owner to a variety of sounds in different environments.

hearing health care provider. Audiologists, hearing aid specialists, and otolaryngologists.

hearing loss. The loss of hearing ability, ranging from mild to profound.

infrared system. A device that transmits amplified sound by invisible light waves to a receiver, thus eliminating background noise and distance problems.

International Symbol of Access for Hearing Loss. A symbol, used worldwide, that identifies locations where communication access is provided.

interpreter. A person who conveys the spoken message to a person with hearing loss by the use of sign language (visible movements of hands, body, and face), orally (silently mouthing the words), or with Cued Speech.

ITC (in-the-canal) aid. The smallest of hearing aids consisting of an earmold and hearing aid as one unit, fitted to the ear canal.

ITE (in-the-ear) aid. A hearing aid consisting of an earmold and hearing aid as one unit, worn in the contour of the outer ear.

lipreading. *See* speechreading.

mastoid. The rear portion of the temporal bone behind the ear.

Ménière's disease. A disease of the labyrinth of the ear, characterized by loss of hearing, ringing in the ears, and dizziness.

monaural. Refers to hearing with one ear.

neck loop. A loop of wire worn like a necklace that creates a magnetic field that can transmit sound when plugged into a portable radio or personal FM or infrared receiver.

otolaryngologist. A medical doctor who specializes in problems of the ear and throat.

otologist. A medical doctor who specializes in problems of the ear.

presbycusis. The slow, progressive type of hearing loss that often accompanies aging.

realtime captioning. The process of producing and projecting onto a screen verbatim dialogue as typed by a court reporter; clear, accurate print that is easily visible to people in large audiences.

relay service. Service that enables text telephone (TTY) users to communicate with non-text telephone users by way of a relay service communications assistant.

residual hearing. The amount of hearing that remains after the occurrence of hearing loss.

sensorineural hearing loss. Also called nerve deafness, a type of hearing loss caused by damage to the inner ear, auditory nerve, or auditory cortex of the brain; it is permanent and usually helped with hearing aids.

Signed English. A form of communication that uses signs in English word order.

sign language. A manual system of communication by which concepts and language are represented visually. Depending on personal preferences, deaf and hard of hearing people in the United States may choose to communicate using the unique grammar and syntax of American Sign Language (ASL) or another variety of signing that uses features taken from ASL and English.

silhouette. An adapter, placed behind the ear and used with a hearing aid equipped with a T-switch, that transmits an FM radio signal to the aid.

speechreading. The interpretation of the spoken message by recognizing the movements of the lips, jaws, and tongue as well as additional cues such as body language, gestures, facial expressions, and conversational context.

telecoil (T-switch). A setting on a hearing aid used in conjunction with a hearing aid-compatible telephone, assistive listening device, and audio loop system that enables the hard of hearing person to hear better by eliminating disturbing background noise and the effect of distance.

telecommunications relay service. *See* relay service.

text telephone. *See* TTY.

tinnitus. Noise in the ears, such as ringing, clicking, buzz-ing, or roaring.

TTY (TDD and text telephone). A telecommunication de-vice that transmits and receives typewritten messages when used in conjunction with a telephone.

Information Resources on Hearing Loss

IN ADDITION to Self Help for Hard of Hearing People, Inc. (SHHH), the organizations listed below provide information of interest to people with hearing loss.

Academy of Dispensing Audiologists (ADA)
3008 Millwood Avenue
Columbia, SC 29205
(800) 445-8629 Voice
www.audiologist.org

ADA represents audiologists who dispense hearing aids as part of their audiological and rehabilitative practice.

American Academy of Audiology (AAA)
8300 Greensboro Drive, Suite 750
McLean, VA 22102
(703) 790-8466 Voice/TTY
(800) AAA-2336
www.audiology.org

AAA is a nonprofit organization for professional audiologists that serves as a forum for exchange of information and ideas in the areas of current research, clinical practices, hearing aid amplification/cochlear implants, and comprehensive rehabilitative intervention for people with hearing loss. AAA provides listings of certified audiologists to the general public.

American Academy of Otolaryngology—Head and Neck Surgery, Inc. (AAO—HNS)

One Prince Street
Alexandria, VA 22314
(703) 836-4444 Voice
(703) 519-1585 TTY
www.entnet.org

AAO—HNS is a nonprofit medical society that represents the majority of otolaryngologists in the United States. AAO—HNS provides patient education leaflets and physician listings to the public.

American Speech-Language-Hearing Association (ASHA)

10801 Rockville Pike
Rockville, MD 20852
(800) 638-8255 Voice/TTY
(301) 897-5700
www.asha.org

ASHA is the professional, scientific, and credentialing organization for audiologists, speech-language pathologists, and speech, language, and hearing scientists. ASHA provides information about communication disorders, as well as listings of certified speech-language pathologists and audiologists to the general public.

American Tinnitus Association (ATA)
PO Box 5
Portland, OR 97207-0005
(800) 634-8978
(503) 248-9985
www.ata.org

ATA is a national champion of tinnitus awareness, prevention, and treatment. ATA provides information about tinnitus and referrals to local hearing professional and support groups nationwide.

Corporation for National and Community Service (CNCS)
1201 New York Avenue, NW
Washington, DC 20525
(202) 606-5000 Voice
(202) 565-2799 TTY
www.cns.gov

CNCS provides opportunities for people of all ages and backgrounds, including those with hearing loss, to participate in community and national service programs through its three streams of service—AmeriCorps, the Senior Corps, and Learn and Serve America.

HEAR NOW
6700 Washington Avenue South
Eden Prairie, MN 55344
(800) 648-4327 Voice
www.sotheworldmayhear.org

HEAR NOW, the United States program of the Hearing Foundation, provides hearing aids to adults and children who are legal residents of the United States, meet financial criteria, and are approved for assistance. HEAR NOW also collects used hearing aids for recycling. All donations are tax deductible.

National Institute on Deafness and Other Communication Disorders (NIDCD) Information Clearinghouse
1 Communication Avenue
Bethesda, MD 20892-3456
(800) 241-1044 Voice
(800) 241-1055 TTY
www.nidcd.nih.gov

NIDCD Clearinghouse is an information service for health professionals, patients, people in industry and business, and consumers, about the areas of hearing, balance, smell, taste, voice, speech, and language. The clearinghouse focuses on the medical and pathological aspects of deafness and other communication disorders, and offers a database of references to journal articles, books, audiovisual materials, brochures, and other educational materials. It also offers information packets, directories, and a newsletter.

National Service Dog Center (NSDC)
580 Naches Avenue, SW
Renton, WA 98055-2297
(800) 869-6898 Voice
(800) 809-2714 TTY
www.deltasociety.org

NSDC, a program of Delta Society, assists people with disabilities to achieve greater independence and surmount barriers in their environment through service dogs. NSDC provides advocacy on behalf of people with service dogs; education regarding service dog issues; information about the selection, training, stewardship, roles, and applications of service dogs; referral to service dog training programs and related resources; and research assistance.

National Temporal Bone Registry (NTBR)
Massachusetts Eye and Ear Infirmary
243 Charles Street
Boston, MA 02114-3096
(800) 822-1327 Voice
(888) 561-3277 TTY
www.tbregistry.org

NTBR is a nonprofit organization that coordinates the procurement of temporal bones upon the death of a donor, maintains a database of all human temporal bone and associated brain tissue in the United States, and disseminates information to the public on temporal bone donation.

Registry of Interpreters for the Deaf, Inc. (RID)
333 Commerce Street
Alexandria, VA 22314
(703) 838-0030 Voice
(703) 838-0459 TTY
www.rid.org

RID provides information about types of interpreting, evaluates and certifies interpreters nationwide, and maintains a list of certified interpreters.

Rehabilitation Engineering Research Center on Hearing Enhancement and Assistive Devices (RERC)
Gallaudet University
800 Florida Avenue, NE
Washington, DC 20002-3695
www.hearingresearch.org

The RERC promotes and develops technological solutions to problems confronting individuals with hearing loss, and it provides information and referral for consumer questions on assistive technology and research.

Rehabilitation Services Administration (RSA)
Office of Special Education and Rehabilitative Services
Room 3329-MES
400 Maryland Avenue, SW
Washington, DC 20202-2551
www.ed.gov/offices/OSERS/RSA/

RSA promotes improved and expanded rehabilitation services for deaf and hard of hearing people and individuals
with speech or language problems; RSA also provides technical assistance to staff at state rehabilitation agencies, other
public and private agencies, and individuals.

APPENDIX B

Statistics on Hearing Loss in the Aging Population

- More than 28 million Americans have a hearing loss; 80 percent of those affected have irreversible and permanent hearing damage.
- More than one-third of the United States population has a significant hearing loss by age sixty-five.
- Sixty percent of people with hearing loss are between the ages of twenty-one and sixty-five.
- Sensorineural damage (damage to the hair cells and cochlea caused by genetics or exposure to noise) is the largest, single form of hearing loss, affecting 17 million Americans.
- At least 15 percent of the United States population is affected by tinnitus.
- Persons older than fifty years of age are twice as likely to have tinnitus.
- Ménière's disease causes bilateral hearing loss in 5 to 20 percent of cases.
- More than 75 percent of people with hearing loss could benefit from using a hearing aid.

These statistics are available on-line from the National Institute on Deafness and Other Communication Disorders web site at www.nidcd.nih.gov.

Index

Academy of Dispensing Audiologists (ADA), 161
accidents, and hearing loss, 21
accommodations, public, 99, 100
Advil, 24
aggressive communication, 85, 86, 138–39
aging: denial of, 2; and hearing loss statistics, 4, 8; and presbycusis, 22; and self-image, 136
AIED (Autoimmune Inner Ear Disease), 19
air travel, 120–22
"Air Travel by People with Disabilities," 121
alarm clocks, 66–67, 95
allergic reactions, 50
ALS. *See* assistive listening systems
American Academy of Audiology (AAA), 161
American Academy of Otolaryngology—Head and Neck Surgery, Inc. (AAO—HNS), 162
American Speech-Language-Hearing Association (ASHA), 162
American Tinnitus Association (ATA), 163
Americans with Disabilities Act of 1990 (ADA), 84, 98–99, 116
amplification: diagnosing the need for, 12–13; and hearing aids, 41–42; and sound recognition, 6; of telephones, 71–72
anatomy, ear, 14–17
anesthetics, reactions to, 77
antibiotics, 24
antidepressants, 30
anvil, 15
aspirin, 23
ASR (Automatic Speech Recognition), 65
assertive communication, 85–88, 139
assistive listening systems, 106–8; mechanics of, 58–59; in places of worship, 109–11; in public accommodations, 117–18; traveling with, 121–22
attentiveness, 90–91
attorneys, 124–25
audio induction loop systems, 59–60
audiogram, the, 37–39
audiologists, 33
auditory nerve, 16
Autoimmune Inner Ear Disease (AIED), 19
Automatic Speech Recognition (ASR), 65
automobile accidents, 21
avoidance, of social situations, 137–38

background noise, 88, 92, 103
balance, 16
barbers, interacting with, 96
barotitis, 122
batteries, hearing aid, 56
BICROS (Bilateral Routing of
    Signals) aids, 45
binaural hearing aids, 47–48
biofeedback, 31
blockage, middle ear, 17
body language, 87
body-worn hearing aids, 45
bone anchored hearing aids
    (BAHA), 47
breathing, relaxation and, 144–46
BTE (behind-the-ear) aids, 9, 44, 48,
    53
built-in telephone amplifiers, 71

C-Print, 65
caffeine, 143–44
caller ID, 75
CAN (computer-assisted note-
    taking), 65
cancer treatments, and ototoxicity,
    24
car travel, 119–20
CART (communication access real-
    time translation), 64–65, 124
CAs (communication assistants),
    73
causes, of hearing loss, 20–22
cellular phones, 75–76
cerumen, 17
chemotherapy, and ototoxicity, 24
churches, hearing in, 109–11
CIC (completely-in-the-ear)
    hearing aids, 45
clarity, 6
cleaning earmolds, 51–52

clerks, court, 124–25
Clinoril, 24
closed captions, 64, 107–8
cochlea, 16, 21
cochlear implants, 76–80
cognitive therapy, 31
communication: aggressive, 38–
    39; assertive, 85–88, 139; break
    down, 11–12, 136; and furni-
    ture arrangement, 91–92; in
    hospitals, 112; importance of,
    151–52; improving, 88–91; in
    restaurants, 105. *See also*
    speechreading; telecommuni-
    cations
communication access realtime
    translation (CART), 64–65
communication assistants (CAs),
    73
complaints, filing, 100
completely-in-the-canal (CIC)
    hearing aids, 45
comprehension: and early signs
    of hearing loss, 1; and listening,
    8; and speechreading, 10, 81
computers, 128–31
conductive hearing loss: defined,
    17; treatments for, 8
consonants, distinguishing
    between, 6, 25
conversation. *See* communication
coping strategies: assertive, 139;
    negative, 137–38; self-help, 140
Corporation for National and
    Community Service (CNCS),
    127–28, 163
costs: of cochlear implants, 79; of
    hearing aids, 53–54
counseling, 30
courtrooms, hearing in, 122–25

CROS (Contralateral Routing of
Signal) aids, 45

decibels: and the audiogram, 37–
39; and stages of hearing loss, 5
degrees of hearing loss, 5–6
denial, 2, 137
diagnosis, 12
diaphragmatic breathing, 145
diet: as cause of tinnitus, 29–32;
for hearing loss, 143–44; for
vertigo treatment, 19
digital hearing aids, 45–46, 53
digital wireless phones, 75
dining out, 102–5
direct audio input aids, 48
directional microphones, 49
disability, denial of, 2
discrimination: and civil rights, 98,
100; tests, 36
disease, and hearing loss, 21
disposable hearing aids, 46–47
dizziness, 19
doctors, 39–41. *See also* health care
providers
dogs, hearing, 69
doorbells, 67–68
drive-thru restaurants, 104
driving, signaling devices for, 119–
20
drugs. *See* medication

e-mail, 74, 130
ear canals, 16
ear-level personal FM receiver, 49
eardrum, the: and conductive
hearing loss, 17; and ear
anatomy, 15; impedance testing
on, 37
earmolds, 50–52

earmuffs, 26
earplugs, 26
ears, 14–17
earwax, 17, 52
eldercare, 132–35
emergency situations: in airplanes, 121; communication
during, 114–15; fire alarms for,
67; and living alone, 95–96
emotional pain: and aging, 133;
associated with hearing loss, 3,
135–36; and fear, 140; tinnitus-
caused, 30
employment: assistive systems
for, 125–28; and discrimination,
98–99
engine noise, 26
environmental noise, 25
eustachian tube, 15
exercise, 144
exhalation, 145

FAA regulations, for disabled
people, 121
family and friends: communicating with, 151; hearing loss effects on, 11; and hereditary
hearing loss, 20; Internet contact with, 130; noticing of
hearing loss, 2, 7
fear, 140
Federal Communications Commission (FCC), 101
feedback, 51
fever, and hearing loss, 21
"fight or flight response," 140, 141
fire alarms, 67
fitting hearing aids, 49–52
FM (Frequency Modulation)
Systems, 61–62

FM receivers, 49
frequency, 6
furniture, rearranging, 92

German measles, 21
Golden Access Passport, 120
guided tours, 119

hair cells, inner ear, 18, 21
hairdressers, interacting with, 96
hammer, 15
hardwired systems, 62–63
head injuries, and hearing loss, 21
headphones, 107
health care providers: for cochlear implants, 79–80; communicating with, 112; importance of seeking, 3; in nursing homes, 133–34; by profession, 33; qualities to look for in, 39–41; for tinnitus patients, 28
health, effects of chronic stress on, 141–42, 144
health insurance, 56
HEAR NOW, 57, 164
Hearing Aid Compatibility Act of 1988, 100–102
hearing aid specialists, 33
hearing aids, 43–52; benefits of, 41–43; choosing a dispenser for, 33, 39–41; determining need for, 8–9; fitting, 49–52; mail-order, 10; myths about, 9; and nerve deafness, 8; purchasing, 52–57; for treating tinnitus, 30
hearing dogs, 69, 165
Hearing Loss: The Journal of Self Help for Hard of Hearing People, 147
hearing tests, 34–39; by health care provider, 32–33; myths about, 9–10

heredity, 20
Hertz, 37–39
high frequencies, hearing erosion at, 6, 25
historic places, tours of, 119
home environments, rearranging, 91–93
homostasis, 144
hospitals, 96, 97–98, 111–16
hotels, 117–18

impedance testing, 37
implantable hearing aids, 47
implants, cochlear, 76–80
in-line amplifiers, 72
incus, 15
induction coil, 70
infrared systems, 60–61
inhalation, 145
inner ear: damage, 18, 21; defined, 16; and ear anatomy, 14–15
International Symbol of Access for Hearing Loss, 97–98
Internet communication, 128–31
"interpreters," 13
intravenous antibiotics, 24
isolation, self-imposed, 137–38
ITC (in-the-canal) hearing aids, 44, 53
ITE (in-the-ear) hearing aids, 9, 44, 53

jaw joint dysfunction, 30–31
judges, 124–25
jury duty, 122–23

labyrinth, 16
large-area assistive listening systems, 59
legal procedures, 125
legal rights, 98–102, 116

legislation, disability-related, 98–102

lighting, speechreading and, 92, 103

lipreading. *See* speechreading

listening, 8

living environments: rearranging, 91–93; solitary, 93–97

loop diuretics, 24

loudness: and comprehension, 6; and stages of hearing loss, 5

low fat diet, 143

low frequencies, 6

M-T-switch, 48

mail-order hearing aids, 10, 57

malleus, 15

masking devices, for tinnitus, 30

mediation, 100

Medicaid, 56

medical help. *See* health care providers

Medicare, 56

medication: and inner ear damage, 21; ototoxic, 22–25; and stress, 144; for treating tinnitus, 30

Ménière's disease, 19

microphones, directional, 49

middle ear, 15, 17

mild hearing loss, 5, 7

mixed hearing loss, 18

moderate hearing loss, 6

motels, 117–18

Motrin, 24

movie theatres, 106–8

mumps, 21

muscle relaxants, and ototoxicity, 24

museum tours, 119

myths, hearing loss, 7–10

narration, oral interpretation of, 83

National Court Reporters Association, 124

National Institute on Deafness and Other Communication Disorders (NIDCD) Information Clearinghouse, 164

national parks, 120

National Service Dog Center (NSDC), 165

National Temporal Bone Registry (NTBR), 165

nerve deafness: introduced, 18; treatments for, 8

noise, 25–27; background, 88, 92; engine, 26; and hearing loss, 21–22; and tinnitus, 29

nonsteroidal anti-inflammatory drugs, 24

nursing homes, 132–35

nutrition, 143–44

officers, court, 124–25

one-on-one communicators, 63

One Voice, 110

oral interpreters, 82–84

otolaryngologists, 33

ototoxic medications, 21, 22–25

outer ear, 14, 15

outpatient procedures, 114

paging systems, 68

pain, emotional vs. physical, 3

passive behavior, 86, 139

Personal Digital Assistants, 129

personal FM systems, 63

personal listening systems, 62–63

pinna, 15, 16

pitch, 6

plane travel, 120–22

portable amplifiers, 72

preadmission, hospital, 111–12
presbycusis, 22
pricing, hearing aid, 53–54
profound hearing loss, 6, 76
programmable hearing aids, 45–46, 53, 54
psychosocial issues, 135–40
public speeches, oral interpretation of, 82
pure-tone air conduction, 36
pure-tone bone conduction, 36

quinine, 24

Rear Window System, 107–8
registration, hotel, 118
Registry of Interpreters for the Deaf (RID), 84, 166
Rehabilitation Act of 1973, 101
Rehabilitation Engineering Research Center on Hearing Enhancement and Assistive Devices (RERC), 166
Rehabilitation Services Administration (RSA), 167
rehabilitation, vocational, 127
relaxation, 144–46; and stress management, 142; for treating tinnitus, 31
religious services, 109–11
rephrasing, 90
residual hearing, protecting, 26
responsibility, assuming, 87–88
rest, 144
restaurants, 102–5
ringing in the ears, 18–19, 27–32
rubella, 21

salicylates, 23

salt intake, 143
self-help, 140
Self Help for Hard of Hearing People. *See* SHHH
self-image, and hearing loss, 136–37
seminars, oral interpretation of, 83
senior care, 132–35
sensorineural hearing loss: defined, 18; implants for, 77; myths about, 8
severe hearing loss, 6, 76
SHHH (Self Help for Hard of Hearing People), 147–150; and legal rights, 101–2; as peer support, 34; and signaling device testing, 69
sight, sense of, 93
sign language, 83
signaling devices, 66–69; and arrangement of living space, 92–93; and living alone, 94–96
sirens, signal devices for hearing, 120
smoke alarms, 67
social situations: and hearing loss, 1; restaurants, 102–5. *See also* communication
sound, and ear anatomy, 16–17
speech discrimination test, 36
speech processors, 79
speech reception test, 36
speechreading, 80–82; myths about, 10; and oral interpretation, 83
spinal meningitis, 21
spouses, communicating with, 13
stapes, 15
statistics, of hearing loss, 4, 169

stirrup, 15
stress: as cause of tinnitus, 31; as "fight or flight response," 140; managing, 141–46
stressors, 142
surgical procedures: cochlear implants, 78–79; communication during, 113–14

T-switch, 42, 48, 70
TDDs, 72–73
telecoil, 42, 70
telecommunications, 69–76; and the ADA, 99; and the Hearing Aid Compatibility Act of 1988, 100–101; in hotels, 118; and the International Symbol of Access for Hearing Loss, 97–98; signaling devices for, 67–68; and the telecoil, 42
Telecommunications Relay Service, 73–74
Television Decoder Circuitry Act of 1990, 101
television listening devices, 63–64, 118
temples, hearing in, 109–11
temporomandibular joint dysfunction, 30–31
tests, hearing, 9–10
theaters, 106–8
therapy: cognitive, 31; drug, 30; tinnitus retraining, 31–32
threshold tests, 36
time management, 143
timers, 67

tinnitus, 27–32; defined, 18–19; treatments for, 29–32
tinnitus retraining therapy, 31–32
TMJ treatment, 30–31
tours, 119
travel, 96, 117–22
TTs, 72–73
TTYs, 72–73, 130
turn signals, 68

U.S. Access Board, 101

vertigo, 19
veterans, and hearing aid eligibility, 57
vibrations, inner ear, 16
vision, 93, 115
visual systems, hearing-assistive, 64–65
visualization, breath and, 145
vocational rehabilitation, 127
voice carry-over (VCO) mode, 72, 74
voice messaging, 74–75
volume control, telephone, 71
volunteer work, 125–28

wake-up devices, 66–67
warning signs, of hearing loss, 1
warranties, hearing aid, 55
wax, ear, 17, 52
work environments, 125–28
work-related hearing loss: accidental, 21; by occupation, 21–22

Xanax, 30